BASS-1

JOHN SEBASTIAN GASKIN

Beginning: Bass Guitar - Music Theory - Sight Reading

Copyright © 2016 by John Sebastian Gaskin

All rights reserved. No part of this book may be reproduced or transmitted in any form without permission in writing from the publisher, including public performance for profit.

Jo-Kin Music, Trinidad and Tobago
jokinmusic@gmail.com

ISBN: 978-976-95914-0-0

Table Of Contents

0 - *Introduction*	*-1*
1 - *The Bass Guitar*	*-2*
2 - *The Positions*	*-6*
3 - *Four Rules*	*-8*
4 - *The Student*	*-10*
5 - *The Fretboard*	*-12*
6 - *Music Theory 101*	*-14*
7 - *Rhythmic Training 101*	*-22*
8 - *Fretboard Basics 101*	*-26*
9 - *Sight Reading 101*	*-32*
10 - *Music Theory 102*	*-34*
11 - *Fretboard Basics 102*	*-42*
12 - *Rhythmic Training 102*	*-48*
13 - *Music Theory 103*	*-52*
14 - *Songs*	*-56*
15 - *References*	*-i*

Dedicated To My Brat.

"You are my Heart, my Life"

0 - Introduction

"The Bass Guitar belongs to the String Instrument family; along with the Harp, Violin, Cello, Sitar, Banjo, Zither, Lute, Cuatro, Mandolin and Guitar."

The **Bass Guitar** has not been around as long as other stringed instruments. The early bass guitar, the acoustic, was the most understated instrument in a band or orchestra, mainly used for accompaniment. Its importance grew when technology of the day gave us the electric bass guitar in the 1930's. With the amplification came a more powerful bottom end.

The bass guitar has helped forge many musical genres such as disco, funk and rock. The bass guitar has moved from being just a supportive instrument to one that can also lead. Players such as Jaco Pastorius, Larry Graham, Louis Johnson, Verdine White, Carol Kaye, Sting, Bernard Edwards, James Jamerson and Gene Simmons have all influenced others with their style and sound.

Students have a choice of learning many style of music on the bass guitar. However, there is no end to the learning of the bass guitar or music. Dedication to your craft is key to being a better musician. This book is all about learning to play the bass guitar. Do not be dismayed, practice slowly and often, and have *fun*. We all started out knowing absolutely nothing and sounding awful.

In this book the student will not only learn the bass guitar but also music theory and sight reading, while learning to play with the pick and fingers.

1 - The Bass Guitar

These days there are multiple varieties and combinations of electric bass guitars, the acoustic bass has remained pure in shape to its original classical self, the upright bass.

Acoustic Bass Guitars (Upright or Double Bass) (Fig.1) are hollow body guitars that do not employ the use of any electronics to amplify their sound. They usually have sound holes on the guitar's front. The metal strings are thicker than those on a guitar. Acoustic bass guitars generate the sound through the sound hole. When a string is played, the sound vibrates in the hollow body of the instrument. It is amplified naturally and sent out through the sound hole.

Electric Bass Guitars (Fig.2) have solid bodies, typically, and use magnetic coils (pick-ups) to generate sound. When the string is played (plucked), the magnetic coil picks up the vibration of the metal string and converts it to electrical energy, which is converted to sound through the use of an amplifier. The thick string vibrates slower and that gives a lower pitched sound.

Some Uprights do employ built in microphones to amplify their sound. The typical bass guitar has four strings but varieties have five and more strings. The Upright bass is the largest of the string family and also employs the use of a 'bow' to play when called for, mainly in classical music.

"The Bass Guitar is a subjective instrument and 'one size does not fit all'. Tone, feel and size are important features in choosing a bass guitar."

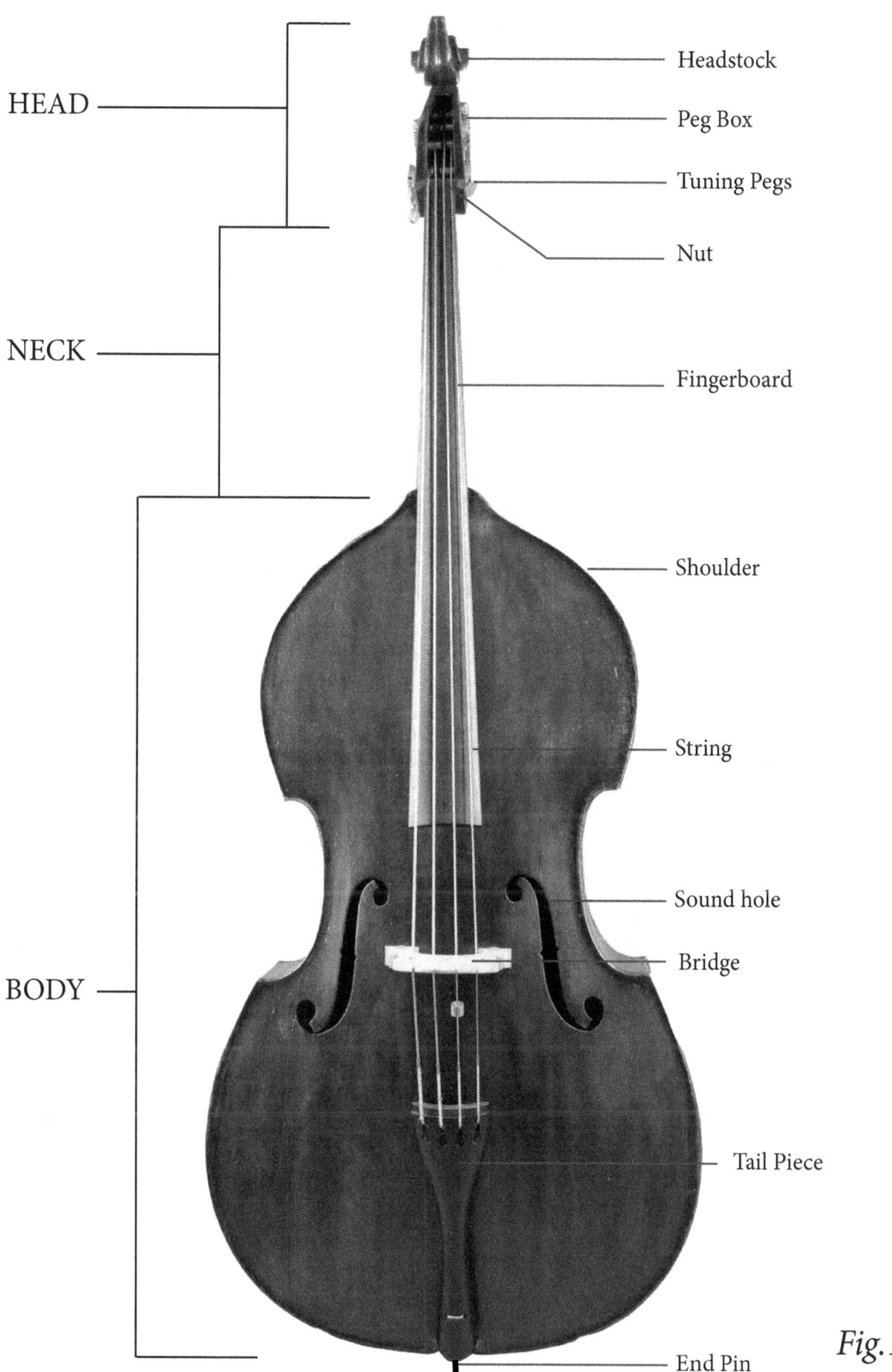

Fig.1

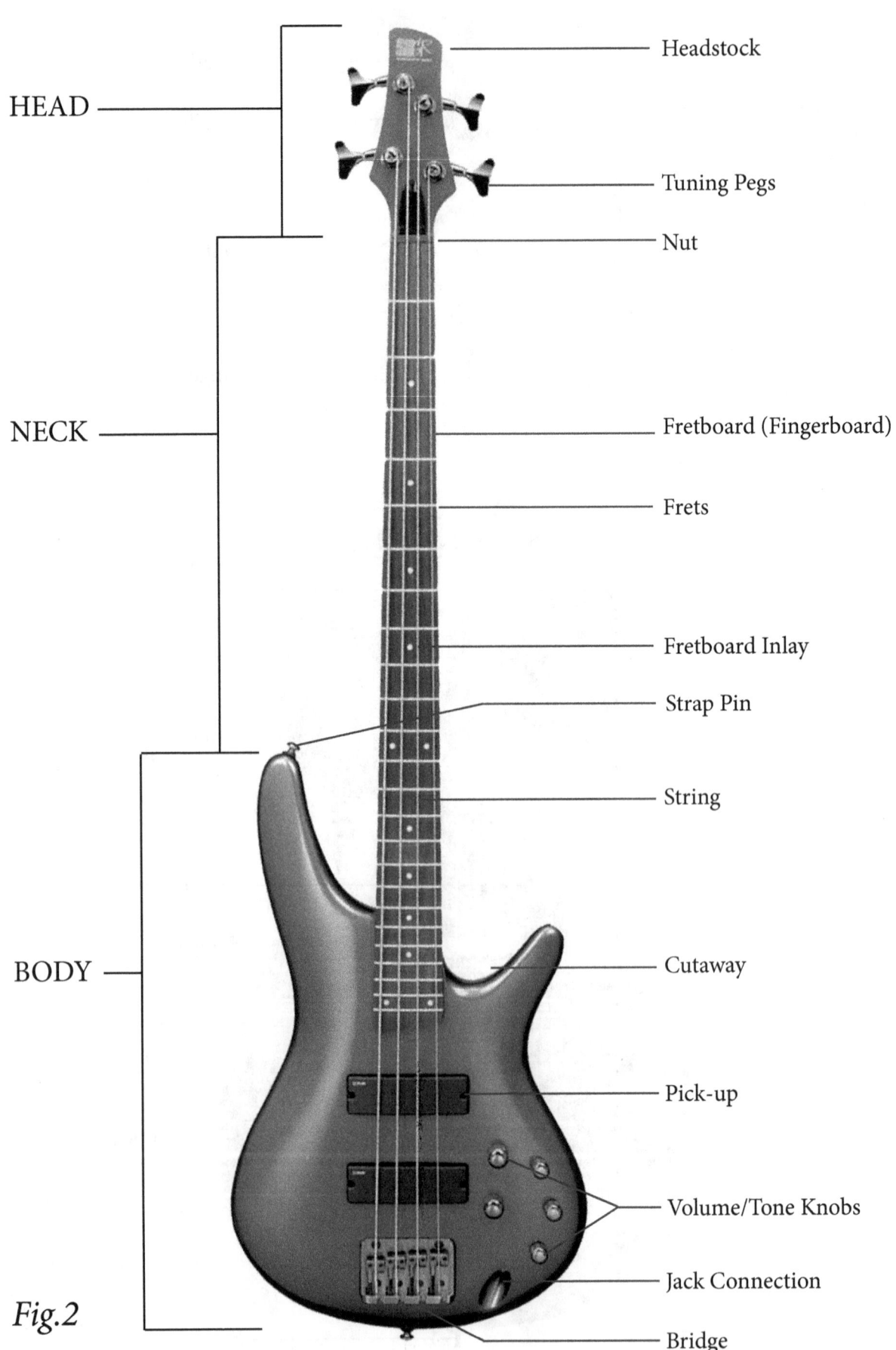

Fig.2

The Bass Guitar has three major sections; the Head, the Neck and the Body (Fig.1 and 2), and may come fretted or fretless.

"The five string bass adds a lower 'B' string as its fifth string above the 'E' string. The six string bass adds a higher 'C' string as its first string below the 'G' string, making the 'B' string the sixth string."

Bridge - The element where the bottom end of the strings are raised to clear the fretboard.

Fretboard - The wooden face of the neck that holds the frets and where the fingers press the strings.

Frets - The metal strips across the fretboard dividing the fretboard, enabling different pitches on each string.

Headstock - The top of the bass guitar that holds the tuning pegs (machine heads).

Nut - The element between the head and neck where the strings pass.

Jack Connection - The hole on the body that allows the guitar cable (jack) to be inserted.

Pick-up - Magnetic coils below the strings on the body that creates electrical energy as the strings vibrate.

Selector Switch - The switch that allows different pickups to be selected.

Sound Hole - The hole in the face of the bass guitar that projects sound.

Strap Pin - The pins on the edges for guitar straps to be anchored.

Tuning Pegs - The machinery holding the top of the strings and wound for proper tuning.

Volume/Tone Knobs - Knobs used for volume and various guitar tones.

2 - The Positions

The Position of the electric bass guitar, while standing, for practice or performance will be decided on according to the style of music to be learnt. The bass guitar may be positioned at the waist area of the player (Fig.3), or lower nearer the knees. The position of the bass guitar may depend on the style of music being played. Heavy Metal bassists typically have their basses nearer their knees. The student should adopt a position that is comfortable. Different basses have different weights so a proper wide strap is important and may be padded to add more comfort.

Fig.3 *Fig.4*

> *"The position of the bass guitar and performer is determined by the style of music to be performed, preference and style of guitar."*

In a sitting position (Fig.4) the bass guitar would be placed on the right leg. The student should sit with both thighs parallel to the floor. This helps to keep the bass and student steady. The bass should be placed just in front of the student's body and angled up from the body of the bass guitar to the head, Figs.3 and Fig.4. The body of the bass should be tilted backward *slightly* and the performer leaning forward to see the front of the bass. The left arm and hand should be angled up towards the neck and the fingers bent towards the fretboard in what I call the 'crab' position. The thumb of the left hand should be vertical on the back of the neck and the pressure point just around the middle of the arch of the neck.

The right arm should be anchored at the elbow on the top of the bass at the middle of the base arch. The right hand should fall and be positioned just at the pickups. The thumb should be anchored to either the edge of the fretboard or the pickup for the fingers to freely play the strings. The thumb also helps hold the pick (Fig.24) to pluck the strings.

The body of the student performer should be upright at all times. The student's head and neck would be bent slightly forward to view the fretboard and strings. Good posture is important for all performers and their endurance in pursuit of proper bass playing. Bassists performing on the Upright bass play in a standing position due to the height of the instrument and which will facilitate playing with a 'bow' on the strings.

3 - Four Rules

Rule #1 - Always tune your bass (Fig.6) before every practice. This will ensure proper tuning every time. You, the student, will also learn to relate the note sounded to the name of the note. Students should hum each note of the open string as they tune. This will be the beginning of the student's ear training.

Rule #2 - Always use a metronome (Fig.5) when practicing. This will ensure that you, the student, develop proper timing. Timing is very important in music. It is truly one of its key components. The metronome should always be set to a slow beat when first starting an exercise. Always start practice with the metronome set at 40 beats per minute.

Rule #3 - Practice all exercises slowly. This is to ensure proper and effective fingering for each exercise. The student can increase speed gradually as he/she becomes adept to the exercises. "It is not about how fast you can play but how well you can play."

Rule #4 - Practice often, one hour a day minimum, including light finger stretches. "Constant practice helps the fingers remember." It is not about having mental recall of the exercises or songs, but the fingers get accustomed to the movements along the fretboard. The muscles of the fingers get a workout, which helps them to remember and makes fingering easier.

"It is not about how fast you can play, but how well you can play. It takes a lot of concentration to play slowly and keep proper timing."

Binding - The decoration around the body of the bass guitar.

Bridge Pins - The pin like elements that holds down the ball end of the strings on the bridge.

Bow - An arched rod with horse hair drawn tightly between its ends.

Fingerboard - This is the fretboard without the metal frets, fretless.

Fingering - The use of the fingers on either hand to play the bass guitar.

Metronome - A device which creates sounds or light pulses with a specifically set timing. It could be sped up or slowed down.

Open Strings - Strings played without the left hand fingers pressing the strings at any fret.

Pick - A small plastic, metallic or synthetic triangular item used to pluck the strings to play the bass guitar.

Tuner - A device used to tune instruments.

Tuning - The process of creating the correct pitches for the open strings by turning the tuning pegs.

 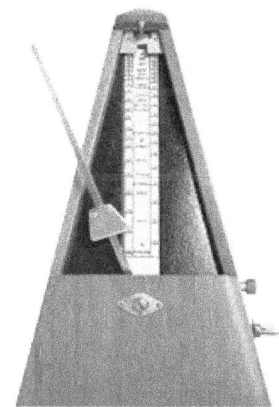    

Fig.5 - Metronomes   *Fig.6 - Tuners*

4 - The Student

In the past there were not many bass guitar teachers and students only learnt to play the bass guitar in whatever style the teacher knew, or as the student wanted. Music theory was basically non-existent, but the student developed his/her ear. It is very important today for the student to learn music theory, sight reading and develop their ear as they learn to play. This is important if one is to take this instrument seriously and wants to earn a livelihood from playing the bass guitar.

The student must learn his instrument. The student must learn each part of his bass guitar physically (Fig.1 and Fig.2). The student must learn each part of his bass guitar musically, every note on every fret (Fig.7). This last item will take some time but students should be diligent in this pursuit. This will help the student in their sight reading, scales and chord locations on the fretboard.

The student should understand each assignment clearly and must practice each assignment diligently before proceeding to the next. The student should be relaxed as this will help with concentration. This book will take the student through elements of music to ensure the student is proficient in bass guitar playing and theory, and versed to communicate with other musicians, no matter what instruments they may play.

"The performer can employ the use of a pick (plectrum) to play the bass guitar, along with playing with the thumb and fingers of the right hand."

For beginning students, I recommend learning first on a four string bass guitar, which will work fine to learn the basics. You can work up to the five and six string basses as you progress and your musical style emerges. The student should be comfortable in both body position and understanding of the work being taught throughout this book.

The student should always set the metronome at 40 beats per minute to start practicing each exercise, and gradually increase the tempo as playing improves. As stated earlier, it is very important for the student to practice slowly.

A reminder to the student, tune the guitar before each practice session. While tuning the student should hum the notes of the open string being tuned. This will reinforce the notes into the memory of the students, and thus ear training begins.

It is not important which tuner or metronome a student buys and uses. They all do the same things. There are even combinations of tuner and metronome. For the beginning student it is recommended not to buy expensive devices. At this stage of learning there is no benefit to having the expensive gadgets. A student should not abuse their equipment. No matter how big or small, respect your instrument. Always clean your equipment after use. This will ensure longer life of the equipment and a better performance every time.

"A good student is one who is willing to learn, practice what they have learnt so that they can improve their status."

5 - The Fretboard

The **Fretboard**, also called the fingerboard, (Fig.7) shows all the notes to be played on the bass guitar. The notes shown in letter form above the nut -E-A-D-G- are the notes of the open strings, tuned. In this book we will be using this standard, most common tuning. There are other types of tuning but they will not be addressed in this book. The numbers above, 4 (thickest) to 1 (thinnest), refers to the string numbering system.

The frets divide the fretboard to accurately produce required pitches from each string. When a string is 'played', it is the action of the left hand finger pressing a string onto the fretboard just behind a specified 'fret' and the right hand finger pulling the string. This 'fret' and the corresponding section of the fretboard preceding it are given the same reference number. So the student may be asked to "play the first string at the fifth fret." In Fig.7 we see that the first string (G string) at the fifth fret produces the pitch 'C'.

The bass is like other string instruments, the same note can be found in different places on the fretboard and on different strings. This opens up a vast array of possibilities and variety of positions from which to play. Notes on the fifth fret are the same as the next open string. From one fret to the adjacent fret gives a chromatic half step interval, and every two frets give an interval of a whole step, F-G or E-F# (Fig.7). At the twelfth fret

"The fretboard comes in several wood options; Ebony, Rosewood and Maple. The different woods give different tones and feel to the performer."

the notes on the strings across the fretboard are the same as the notes of the strings played 'open'. As such, the notes on the thirteenth fret are the same as those on the first fret and so on, the fretboard repeats.

"The Fretboard of the bass is set up chromatically. Plucking a string from one fret to an adjacent fret creates a half step interval."

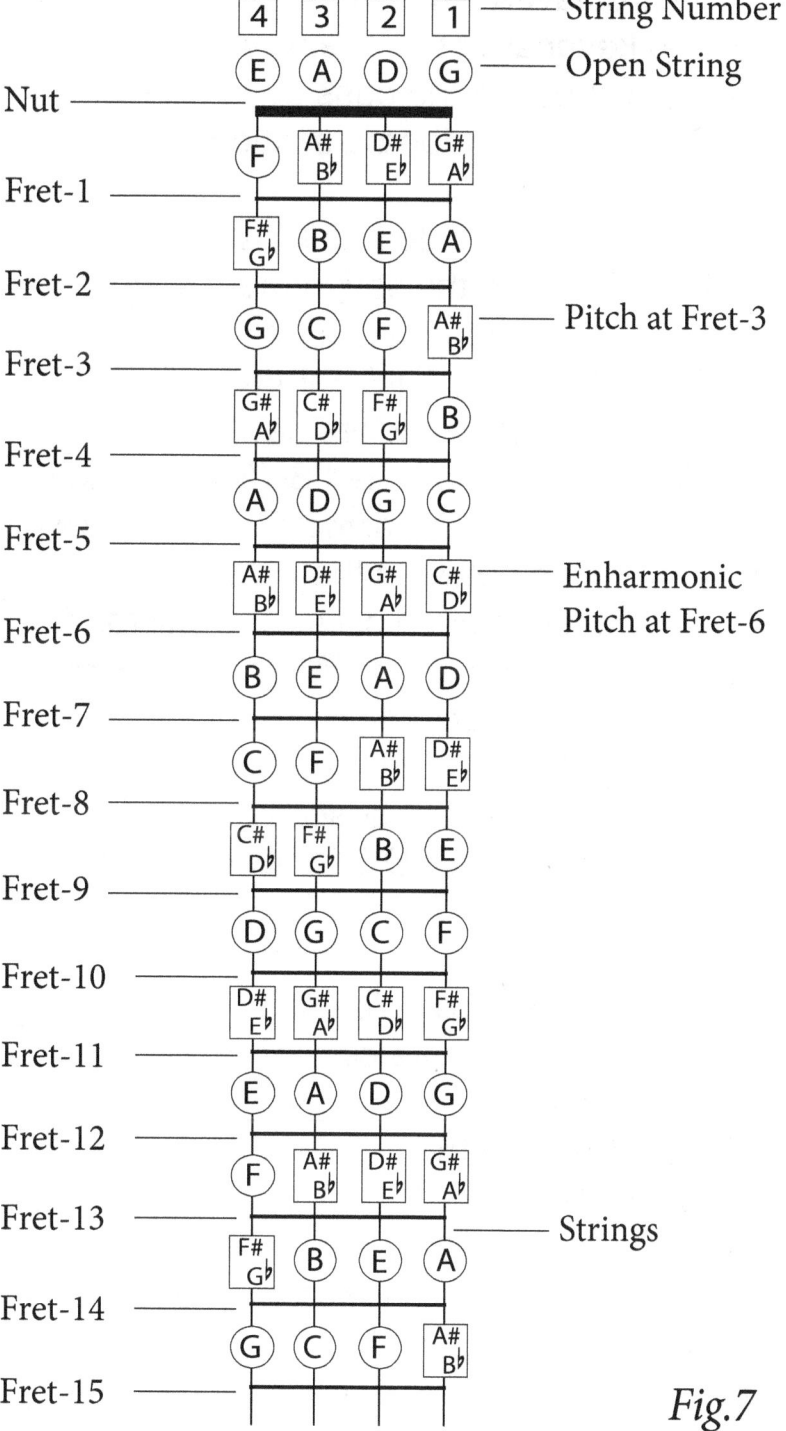

Fig.7

6 - Music Theory 101

There are seven natural pitches in music: **A-B-C-D-E-F-G**. These pitches repeat themselves every eight pitch creating higher or lower octaves. This can be easily seen on a piano keyboard but not easily on the guitar. These pitches, on the bass guitar, are shown in circles in the Fretboard section (Fig.7).

The **Chromatic Scale** has all twelve musical pitches. They are the seven mentioned above plus five intermediary pitches: A-**A#(B♭)**-B-C-**C#(D♭)**-D-**D#(E♭)**-E-F-**F#(G♭)**-G-**G#(A♭)**-A. All intermediary pitches have two names, A# (A-sharp) is also called B♭ (B-flat). They are referred to as **Enharmonic**. There are no sharps or flats between the notes B-C and E-F. However, they do occur. We will touch on them as we go along. When pitches are indicated in the ascending order **Sharps** are used: A-A#-B-C-C#-D-D#-E-F-F#-G-G#-A. When indicated in the descending order **Flats** are used: E-E♭-D-D♭-C-B-B♭-A-A♭-G-G-F-E♭.

"Do not use sharps and flats together. This will create confusion when working out the key of a composition and chord qualities."

Many instruments employ other keys, as with the B♭ trumpet and the clarinet in A. Music for the bass guitar is written in the **Bass Clef**, different from the treble clef of the guitar but is also written in the key of 'Concert C'. The bass clef is also referred to as the 'F' clef or sign (Fig.9). We will show other clef signs in this book as we teach certain musical features. We will not be teaching the many musical clef signs in this book.

"Enharmonic tones carry two names such as A♯ and B♭, but have the same sound (frequency and pitch)."

Accidentals - Signs indicating whether notes are 'sharp-(#)', 'flat-(♭)' or 'natural-(♮)' in pitch.
Chord - Several notes played together for accompaniment, as soloist or group.
Chromatic - Half step intervals between notes. B-C-C#-D-D#-E-F.
Clef - The sign indicating the range in which musical notes occur and indicative of the musical tuning of the instrument.
Harmony - When more than one note is played at the same time.
Key - The note scale used in a composition.
Measure - Section of the staff between the vertical bar lines.
Melody - When one note is played after the other respective of pitch.
Note - The symbol on the musical staff, on the line or in a space indicating pitch.
Octave - Eight musical notes, the seven musical notes and the root repeated at the eight scale tone.
Pitch - The frequency of a note, the faster the frequency the higher the pitch.
Rests - The symbol on the musical staff indicating when not to play (rest).
Scale - A series of notes played in order of ascending or descending starting and ending on the key note.
Staff - The five horizontal lines creating a musical score (sheet music) where notes are placed.
Time Signature - The two numbers, one above the other, at the beginning of the staff after the clef sign.

There are different notes in music and they have their corresponding rest signs. The Whole note (o) represents four beats. Two Half notes (𝅗𝅥) equal one whole note. Two Quarter notes (♩) equal one half note. Two Eight notes (♪) equal one quarter note. Two Sixteenth notes (𝅘𝅥𝅯) equal one eight note (Fig.11 and Fig.12). The Quarter note is the most common beat in music.

The beat in an actual music score will be determined by the time signature. In 6/8 timing the eight note represents one beat in that musical composition. We will continue with timing and rhythm in the following section of Rhythmic Training. We will not be looking at thirty-second notes or rests in this book. For the student's information, two thirty-second notes or rests equal one sixteenth note or rest.

Rests have values similar to notes. There are Whole rests, Half rests, Quarter rests, Eight rests, Sixteenth rests (Fig.13). Think of rests as chances to catch your breadth.

The notes on the Bass Clef (Fig.10) start from 'E' on the **Ledger Line** below the staff and goes above the staff. The notes that fall above or below the staff will be written on or between ledger lines (Fig.9). The shaded notes show the open strings pitches. The bass guitar sounds an octave lower than written. The notes go up alphabetically, no skipping; E-F-G-A-B-C-D-E +. Reading from right to left and as such, bottom to top. The notes on the lines in the staff are G-B-D-F-A.

"The top number of the time signature indicates the number of notes in the measure. The bottom number indicates type of note."

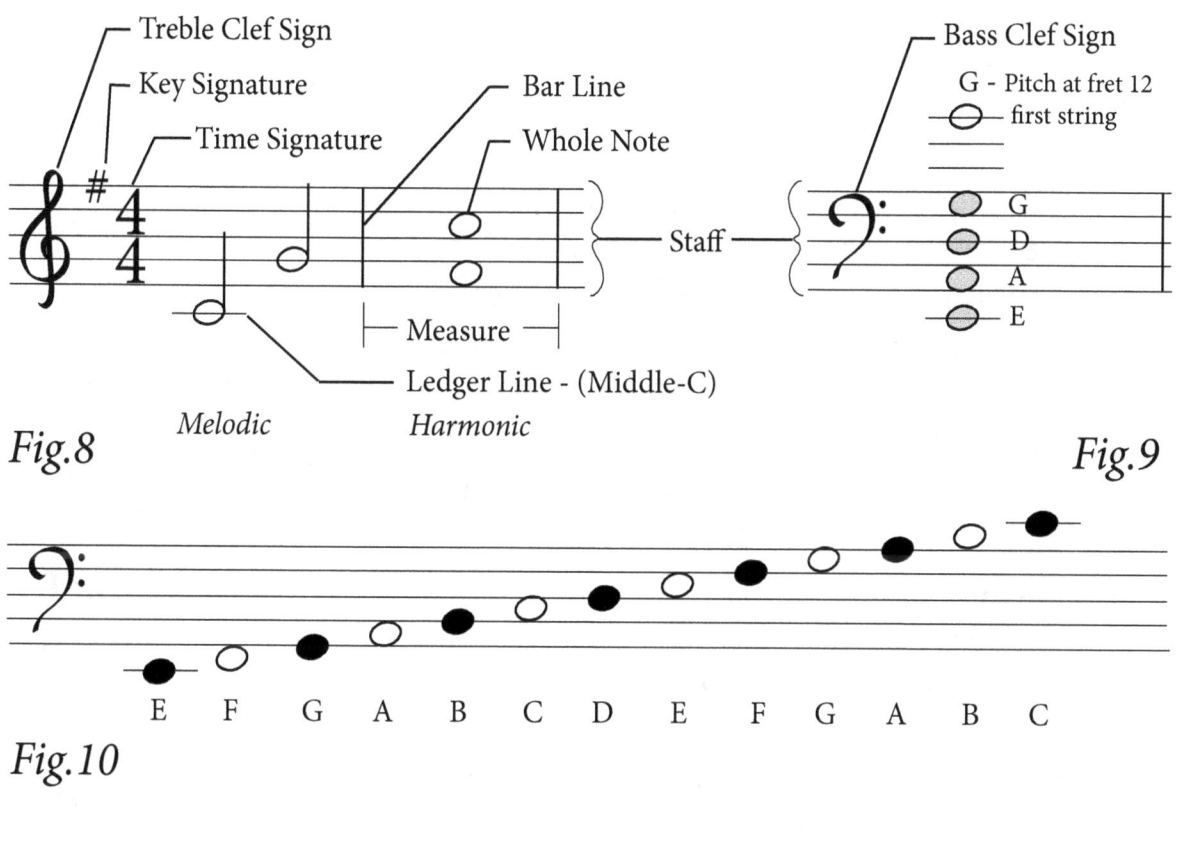

Fig.8 Fig.9

E F G A B C D E F G A B C

Fig.10

1 whole note = 2 half notes = 4 quarter notes = 8 eight notes

Fig.11

8 sixteenth notes = 4 eight notes = 2 quarter notes = 1 half note

Fig.12

The notes in the spaces are A-C-E-G. The notes on the line and those in the spaces skip alphabetically (Fig.10). Once you know where 'C' is on the bass you can find the other notes.

We mentioned earlier in this section that there are no sharps or flats between B-C and E-F. As mentioned, they do happen. If you look at the F# Major scale on the next page (Fig.14) you will see an E# note. The note cannot be called F as there is already an 'F' in the scale (F#). This can also be seen in the G♭ scale where C♭ occurs. The alphabet has to be followed and no doubling of letters can occur. The root notes in the scales with sharps, C-G-D-A-E-B-F#, have intervals of a 'perfect fifth' from note to note, and is referred to as the **Circle of Fifths**. The root notes in the scales with flats, C-F-B♭-E♭-A♭-D♭-G♭, have intervals of a 'perfect fourth' from note to note, and is referred to as the **Cycle of Fourths**.

An **Major Scale** is made up of eight pitches (notes) with intervals of five whole steps and two half steps (Fig.15). In Fig.14 you see some of the Major Scales in music, those with sharps and those with flats occurring. A Major Scale is also known as a **Diatonic** Scale, from the **Tonic**. Other scales have different intervals between pitches and may not start on the Tonic, which differentiate each scale. Intervals are measured from first (root) pitch to every other pitch in the scale and are linked to the distance, whole step or half step (semi-tone), between each pitch.

"All notes and rests should be played and held for their required duration as written. Only when there are accents on the notes that their duration changes."

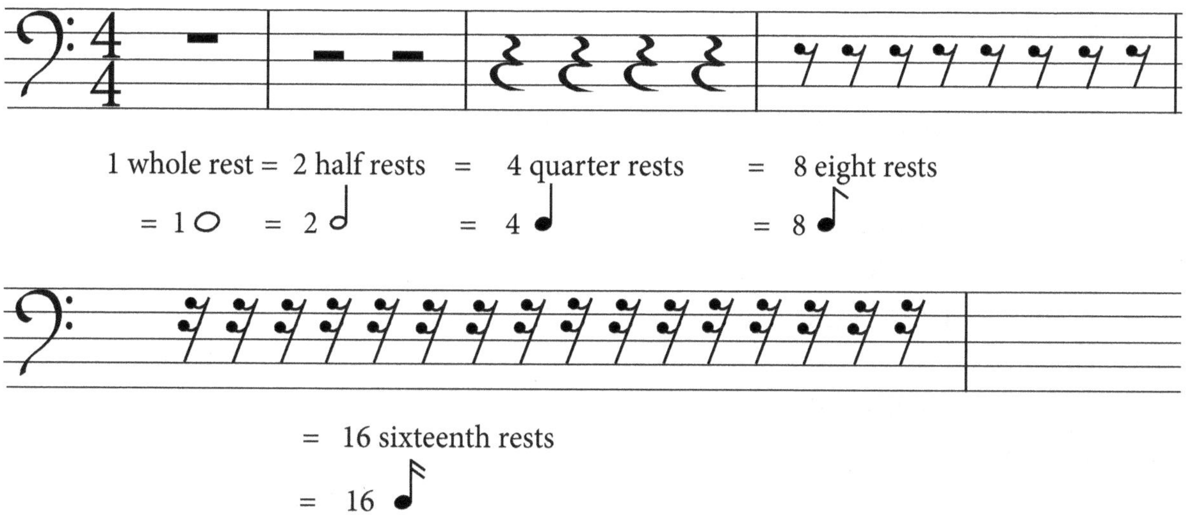

1 whole rest = 2 half rests = 4 quarter rests = 8 eight rests
= 1 𝅝   = 2 𝅗𝅥   = 4 ♩   = 8 ♪

= 16 sixteenth rests
= 16 ♬

Fig.13

MAJOR SCALES:

Root	Sharps or Flats	Scale Notes
C	None	C-D-E-F-G-A-B-C
G	1 Sharp	G-A-B-C-D-E-F#-G
D	2 Sharps	D-E-F#-G-A-B-C#-D
A	3 Sharps	A-B-C#-D-E-F#-G#-A
E	4 Sharps	E-F#-G#-A-B-C#-D#-E
B	5 Sharps	B-C#-D#-E-F#-G#-A#-B
F#	6 Sharps	F#-G#-A#-B-C#-D#-E#-F#
F	1 Flat	F-G-A-B♭-C-D-E-F
B♭	2 Flats	B♭-C-D-E♭-F-G-A-B♭
E♭	3 Flats	E♭-F-G-A♭-B♭-C-D-E♭
A♭	4 Flats	A♭-B♭-C-D♭-E♭-F-G-A♭
D♭	5 Flats	D♭-E♭-F-G♭-A♭-B♭-C-D♭
G♭	6 Flats	G♭-A♭-B♭-C♭-D♭-E♭-F-G♭

Fig.14

As mentioned previously, from one fret on the bass guitar to an adjacent fret is a measurement (distance) of a semi-tone, or half step. Any distance two fret away creates a whole step measurement (F-G, B-C#). Fig.15 shows the distance between notes in the B♭ scale. In a Major scale the distance (measurement) between notes are listed as 'W-W-H-W-W-W-H' (W=whole steps and H=half steps or semi-tone).

The other intervals shown in Fig.15 are those from the root note to other notes in the scale. From B♭ (root) to C (2nd) is an interval of a Major Second (one whole step or two half steps). From B♭ to D (3rd) is an interval of a Major Third (two whole steps or four half steps). From B♭ to E♭ (4th) is an interval of a Perfect Fourth (two whole steps and a half step). B♭ to F (5th) is an interval of a Perfect Fifth (three whole steps and a half step). From B♭ to G (6th) is a Major Sixth (four whole steps and one half step). B♭ to A (7th) is an interval of a Major Seventh (Five whole steps and one half step). B♭ to B♭ (8th) is an interval of an Octave (Six whole steps, or broken down is five whole steps and two half steps). The same pitched note played twice is an interval called a Unison.

With this information anyone can build a major scale off of any note in music. This information will take time to understand and learn. So, practice, practice, practice. Go over parts of the lessons as you need to. Always remember two half steps (two semi-tones) are equal to one whole step.

"Chords (root, third and fifth) built from any diatonic note of a particular scale should always have notes from that particular scale. The root of the chord is the note the chord is built from, different from the scale root."

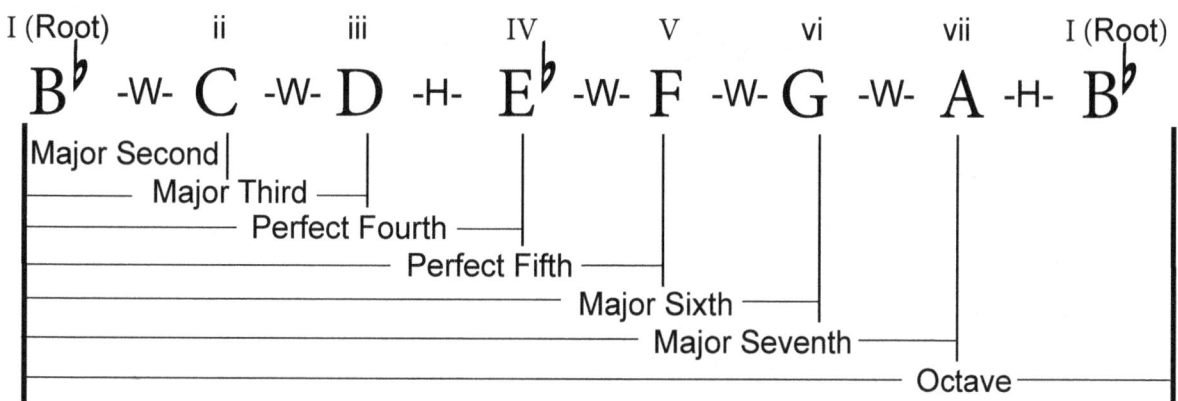

Fig. 15

Arpeggio - Also called Broken Chord, is the playing of the notes of a chord in sequence, one after the other.

Bar Lines - Vertical lines on the musical staff separating measures.

Beat - The musical pulse of a composition.

Dotted Note - A Note with a Dot just after it adds half the value of that note back on to the note.

Interval - The musical reference to distance (measurement) between notes.

Inversion - A chord with different notes in the bass or lowest register, other than the root note.

Ledger Line - The short line above or below the staff where notes are shown.

Progression - A series of chords played one after the other.

Root - The note a scale or chord is built on.

Strum - Playing a number of strings at the same time.

Tie - The line connecting notes to each other that allows the duration of the first note to be added (tied) to the second note.

Triad - A chord with three notes.

7 - Rhythmic Training 101

Knowing the different musical notes, rests and their values are important to learning rhythm. Practice is the other important factor. We have learnt the notes and their values in the Music Theory 101 section. In this section we will not be concentrating much on the bass. This section is about rhythm, so sounding the note and tapping the beat matching the metronome is to be performed.

In the exercises in this section we show the drum staff. There are no pitch values in this staff just note values. Here we are using 4/4 timing, four quarter notes per measure. Each quarter note is a beat. The student should set the metronome to 40 and count the beats slowly, 1-2-3-4, 1-2-3-4,1-2-3-4. All notes are sung or played for its required duration.

In Fig.16 the beat and quarter note are the same so the student should be sounding and counting 1-2-3-4, 1-2-3-4, 1-2-3-4, with the metronome. In Fig.17 two eight notes equal a quarter note beat. The student should be sounding 1-&-2-&-3-&-4-&, where the '&' is on the upbeat. In Fig.18 the half note equals two quarter note beats. The notes occur on the first and third beats and must be held for its duration, the full two beats. In Fig.19 the whole note equals four quarter note beats and should be held for the entire measure. In Fig.20 four sixteenth notes equal one quarter note beat. The student should sound the four notes in the space of each beat.

"I advise anyone who is learning to read music to get the book, 'Rhythmic Training' by Robert Starer. It is a great book."

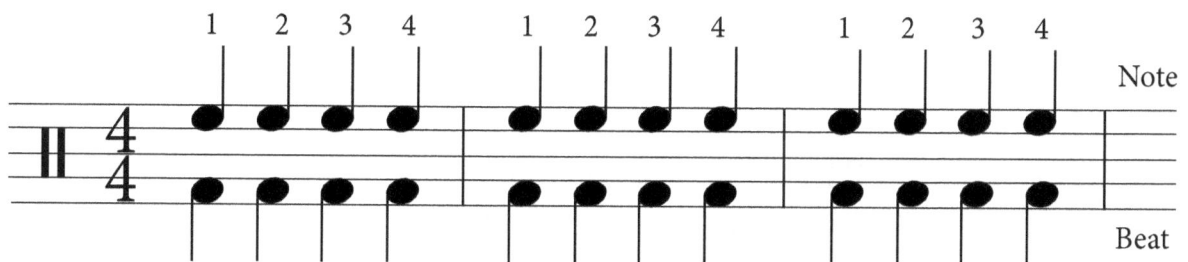

Fig.16

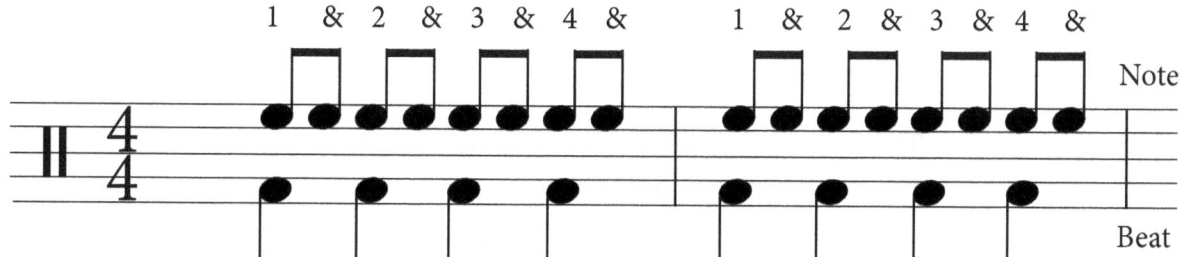

Fig.17

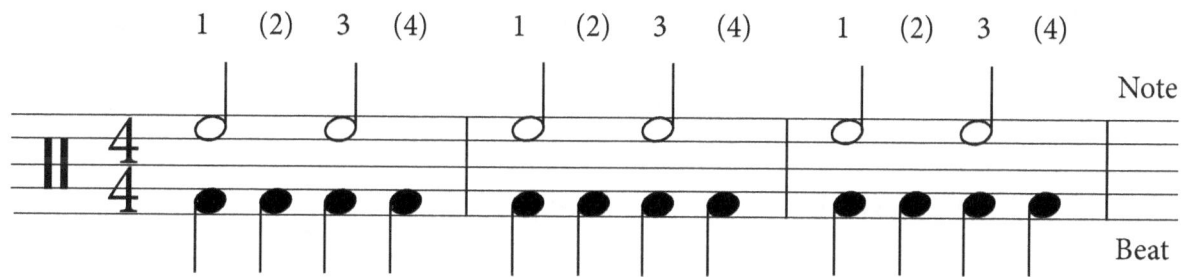

Fig.18

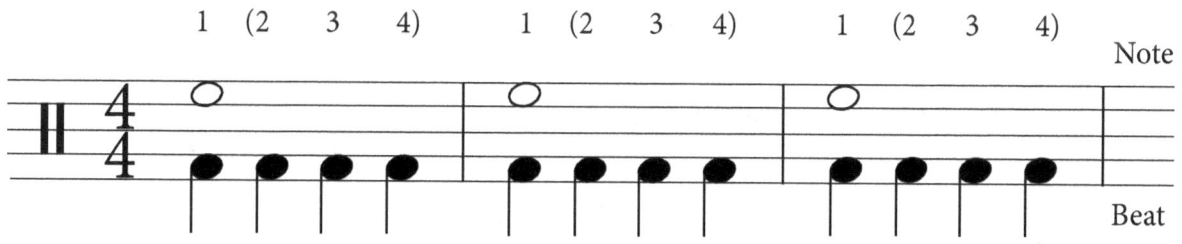

Fig.19

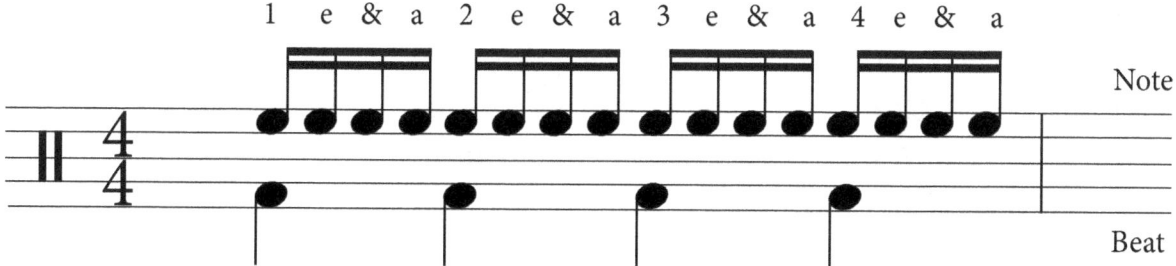

Fig.20

Practice each exercise until it is well understood and accomplished before moving to the next. In Fig.21 the notes are mixed to provide some challenge for you, the student. As always go slowly with the metronome on 40 beats per minute. Go back to the previous exercises if something poses an issue to play or follow properly.

The notes in Fig.21 may be played on the bass guitar. If the student is comfortable with the exercise then playing the notes using one single note on the bass guitar can be a plus. You will also be practicing your playing techniques, pressing the first string at the first fret with the index finger of the left hand. For fingerstyle playing the student shall pluck the notes with the index (i) and middle (m) fingers using alternating strokes. Playing with the pick the student shall play alternating down and up strokes. Go slowly. More will be discussed about fingering in the following Fretboard Exercises 01 section.

We have been told in the Music Theory 101 section about the dot after a note and the note 'tie'. In Fig.22 the exercise adds these values to the score making it even more challenging to the student. This exercise needs even more concentration, and practice, practice slowly. You should not be dismayed or despondent if it takes a while to master these exercises. Be patient and take your time. Good things will happen. Once the student can play these exercises clearly and efficiently, reading music will become that much easier.

"If possible sound the notes using a syllable like 'LA', while trying to tap the beat with your hand or feet. Again, practice slowly."

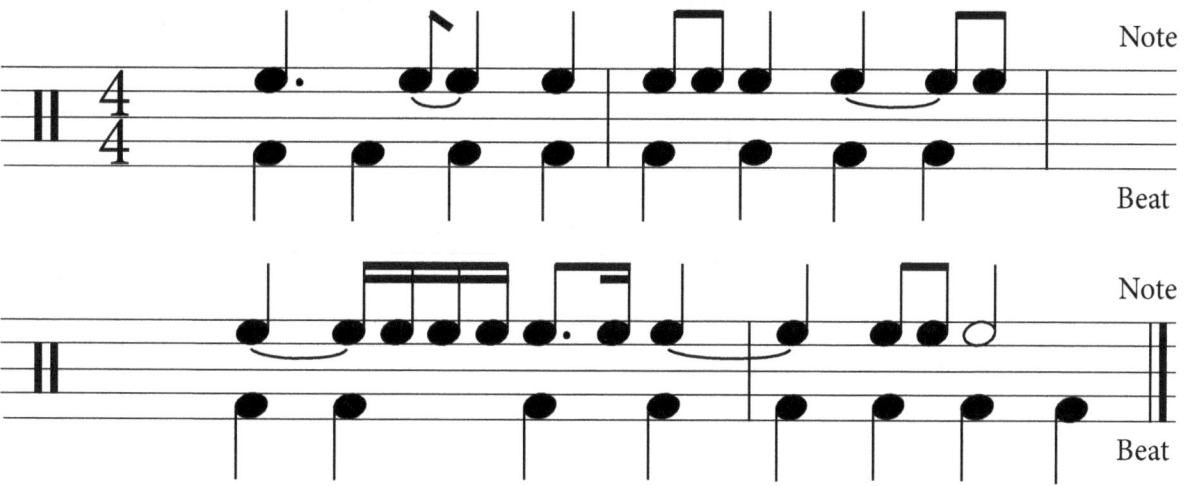

Fig.21

Fig.22

8 - Fretboard Basics 101

Students will learn to play the bass guitar with both their fingers (fingerstyle), and the pick (plectrum). As a student progresses then a decision would be made to play with just the fingers and/or pick. This will be determined mainly by the style of music the student wants to concentrate on and be proficient at.

FINGERSTLYE:
Each finger has a designation in music. The right hand has a letter per finger, and the left has a number per finger, except the thumb (Fig.23). This tells the student which finger to play and where.
The left hand fingers press the strings at the frets to give specific pitches. The right hand fingers pluck the strings to give sound. The strings should be played with the fingertips of the right hand. There are others who are trained to play the strings with fingertips and nail. Nails on the left hand should be clipped low. Nails on the right hand should be in line with the fingertips and properly manicured. The thumb on the right hand is anchored on a string, pickup or side of the fretboard. The fingers of the right hand are pointed slightly towards the bridge of the bass guitar. The fingers will provide either a **Rest Stroke** or **Free Stroke**, and the student gets the next finger to be used into position and 'prepared' to play the next note. Left handed players shall use a reverse reading of the hands.

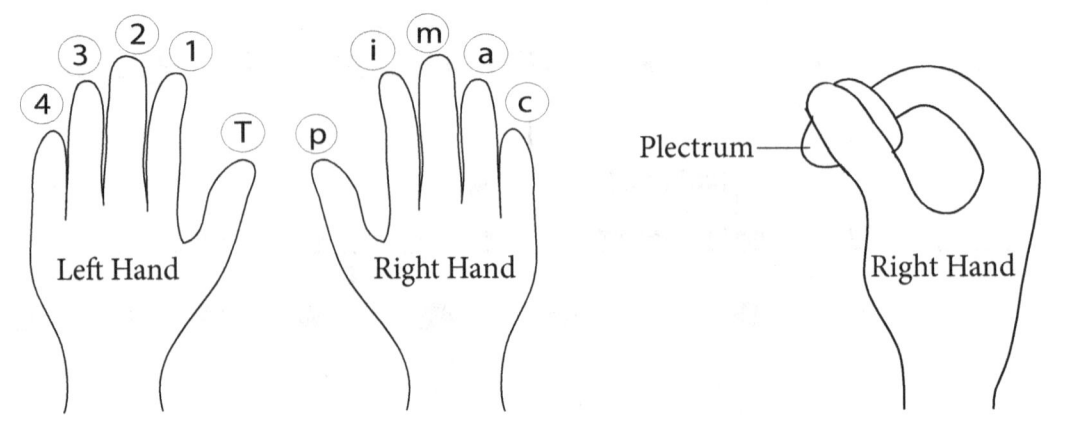

Fig.23   Fig.24

Free Stroke - The process of playing a string with a finger and not resting the finger on any string after playing.
Mute - To dampen, not sound, a string by slightly touching it with one of the left hand fingers, or right palm.
Rest Stroke - The process of playing a string with a finger and resting the finger on an adjacent string after playing.

PLECTRUM STYLE:
While fingerstyle is mainly used to play the bass, the plectrum adds a different tone/attack and comes in many shapes, materials and thicknesses. The student will decide which pick he/she is comfortable with and the tone it produces. All picks no matter what size or shape have at least one point. This point is used to strike the strings. The pick is positioned on the index finger with the point in the direction the finger is pointed. The thumb is then positioned over the pick with the thumb pointed perpendicular to the index finger, creating a cross with the two fingers (Fig.24). How firmly you grip the pick will depend on your style and feel, which will create your own tone and voice on the bass guitar. The other fingers are to be in a closed position, out of the way of the strings. The picking hand should not touch the body of the bass guitar, some bassists do. The student shall use alternate upstroke (U) (∨) and downstroke (D) (⊓) picking using the plectrum starting with the down stroke unless noted otherwise. All picking movement shall employ the wrist and not the elbow.

"The numbers on the fingers of the left hand represent the numbers and the placement of the fingers on the fretboard. See Fig.23, Fig.26A and Fig.27A."

HYBRID PICKING:
The art of using both plectrum and fingers to simultaneously or alternatively pluck the strings.

The following exercises are drills and must be diligently practiced. The exercises show alternate picking on each string, see the information above the staves. Tune the bass guitar and set the metronome to 40. Repeat until the exercises are played comfortably, smoothly and in time with the metronome. The notes should be even in rhythm, tone and volume when done correctly.

Exercise 1:
In Fig.25 the student shall pluck the open first string (G) until the notes are played comfortably in alternate pattern and with each stroke matching the beat of the metronome.

Exercise 2:
In Fig.26 and Fig.26A, the student shall press the first fret on the first string with the first finger and pluck the string four times; then press the second fret with the second finger and pluck four times; then press the third fret with the third finger and pluck four times; and finally, press the fourth fret with the fourth finger and pluck four times. In Fig.27 and Fig.27A, the student shall press the first fret on the second string with the first finger and pluck the string four times; then press the second fret with the second finger and pluck four times; then press the third fret with the third finger and pluck four times; and finally, press the fourth fret with the fourth finger and pluck four times. Then do the same on the third and fourth strings.

Exercise 3:
Play the notes in exercise 2 backwards, from the fourth fret going back to the first fret on each of the four strings starting on the first string.

Exercise 4:
Play the notes in exercise 2, from the fourth string down to the first string, and from the first fret to the fourth fret on all four strings.

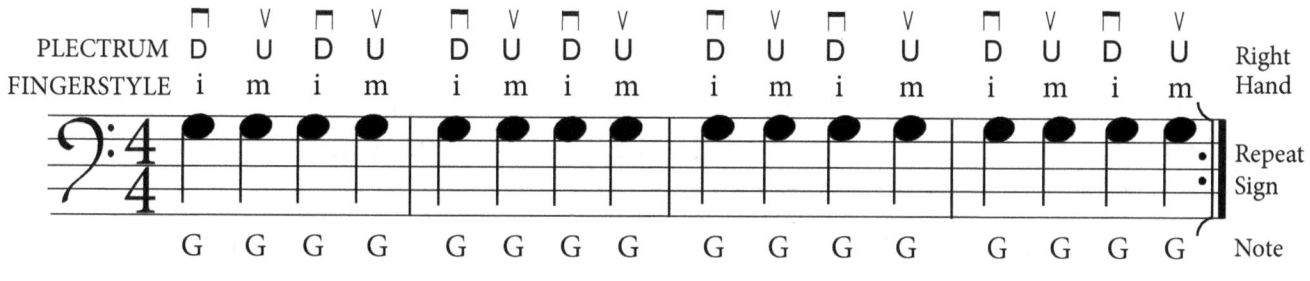

Fig.25

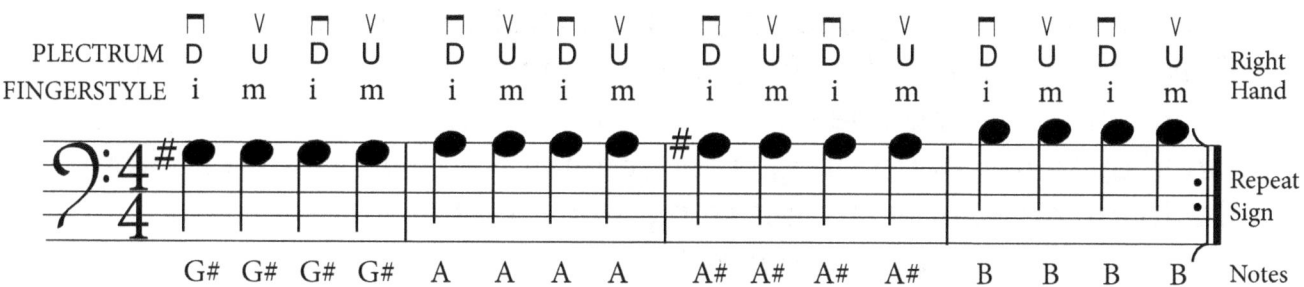

Fig.26

Fig.26A *Fig.27A*

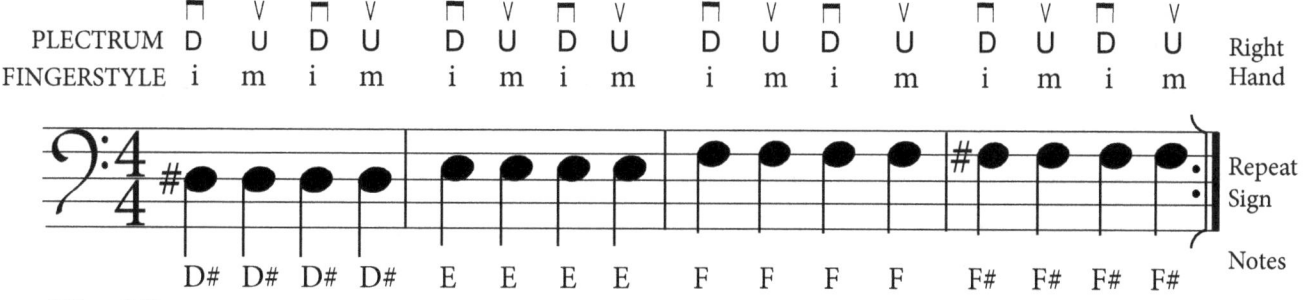

Fig.27

Exercise 5:
Play the notes in exercise 2, starting on the first string and going from the first fret to the fourth fret; then jumping to the third string and playing from the first fret to the fourth; then jumping to the second string and playing from the first fret to the fourth; and then jumping to the fourth string playing from the first fret to the fourth.

Exercise 6:
In Fig.28 you will play one note only per fret instead of four times. Play one note on the first fret, one note on the second fret, one note on the third fret and one note on the fourth fret, going from the first string up to the fourth string. Then reverse the exercise and go from the fourth string down to first string, from first fret to fourth fret on each string, playing once per fret.

Exercise 7:
In Fig.29 play the notes one per fret (as in exercise 6), this time alternating the frets, going from the first fret to the third fret then to the second fret and to the fourth fret, and from the first string up to the fourth. Then reverse the exercise and go from the fourth string back down to the first string alternating the frets on each string.

Exercise 8:
Play the notes one per fret (as in exercise 6), also alternating the frets, this time going from the first fret to the fourth fret to the second fret and then to the third fret. Again go from the first string up to the fourth and then reverse the exercise and go back down to the first string.

These exercises not only gets you to practice your right and left hand techniques, but also allows you to start looking at the notes on the staff and adds an informal introduction into sight reading. Before going to the next exercise make sure that you are playing the exercise smoothly and in time with the metronome, and once that is achieved you could increase the speed of the metronome and practice to faster speeds.

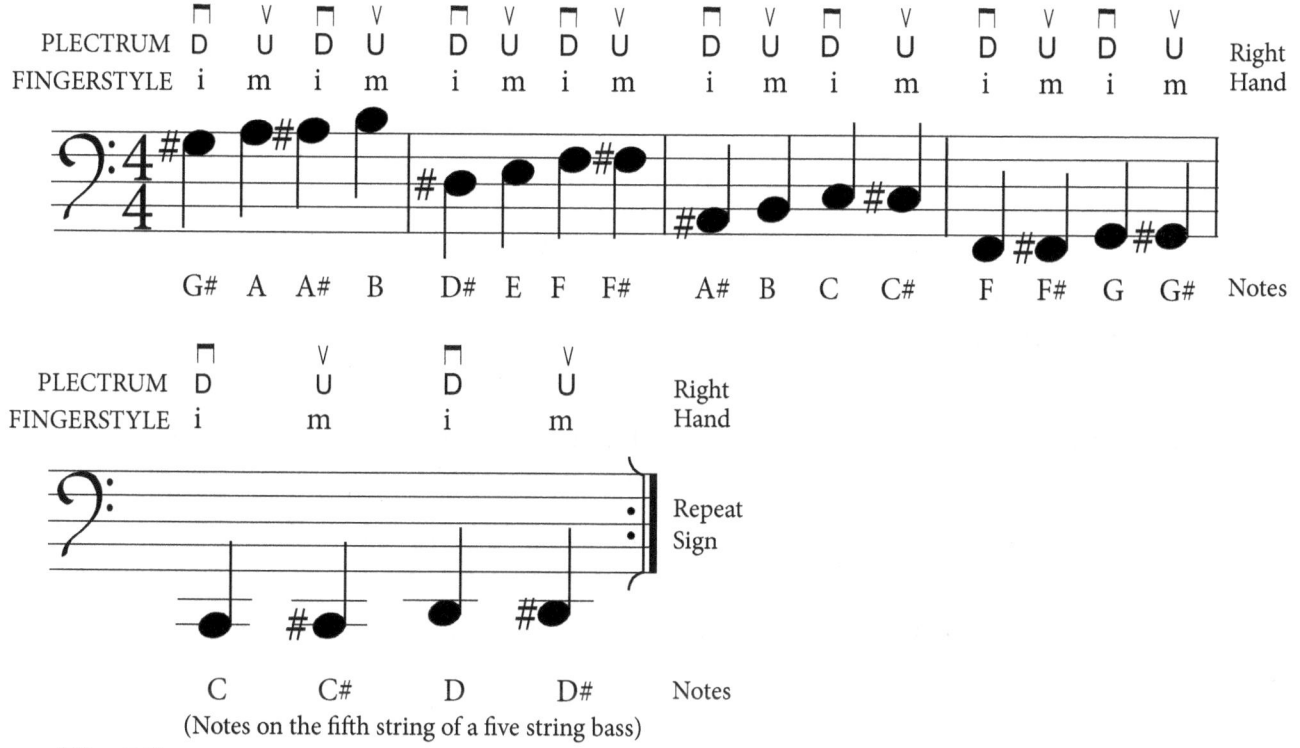

Fig.28

Fig.29

9 - Sight Reading 101

You have learnt the musical notes and have touched on the notes on the first four frets of the fretboard. You have also learnt left and right hand techniques. Now we shall combine them all in this section. In the following exercises are short melodies of songs which you will sight read and play. Most of the melodies you may be familiar with, so you may already have an idea of the melodies. You can go back to any section to review if you run into a mental block. As always, tune your bass guitar and put the metronome on 40 before you begin, take your time and concentrate, you cannot rush these. We all started the same way, not knowing how to play. Hum the pitches you are playing as you associate them with their names.

Baa Baa Black Sheep

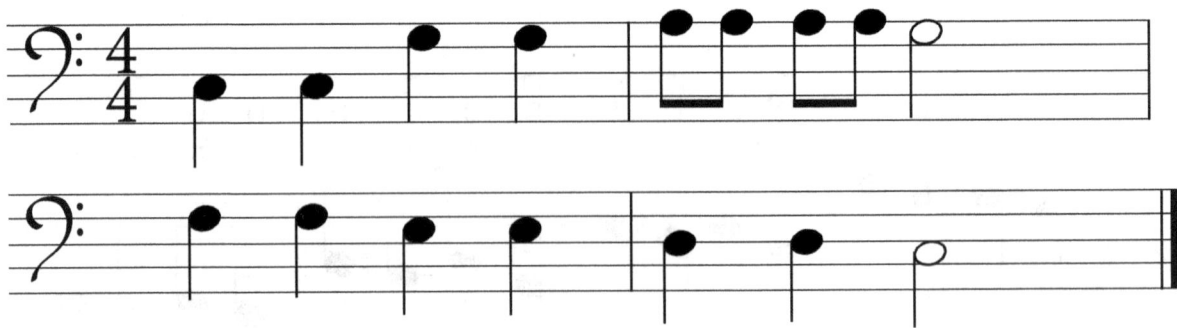

Fig.30

Jingle Bells

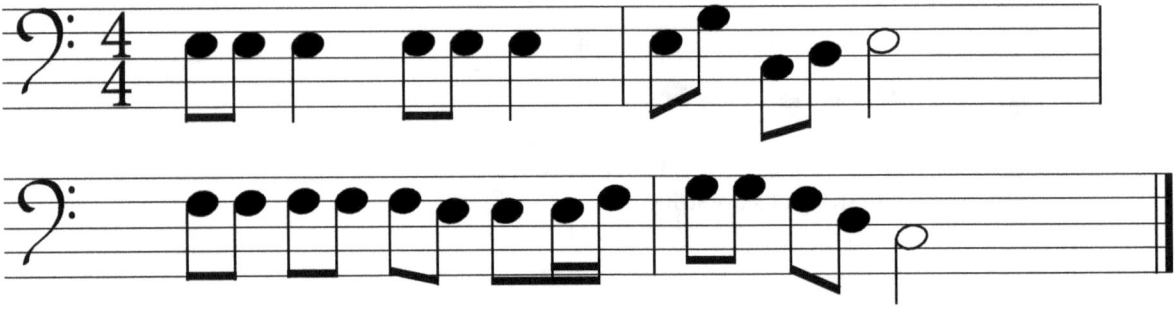

Fig.31

Mary Had A Little Lamb

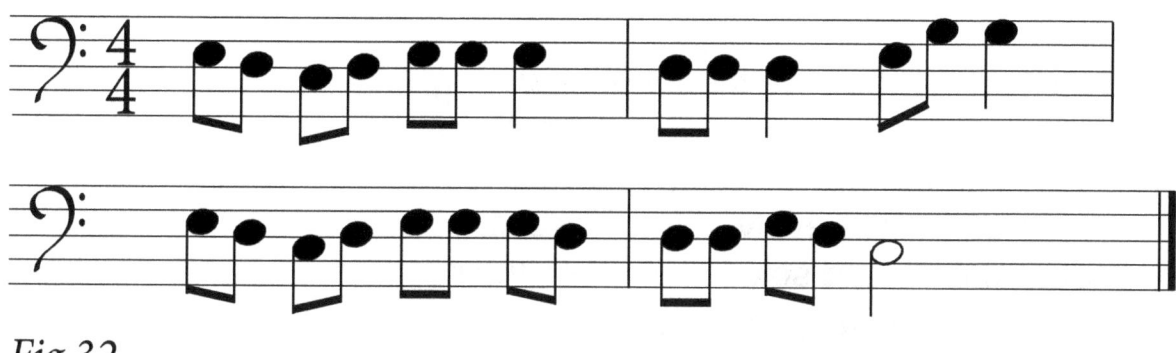

Fig.32

This Old Man

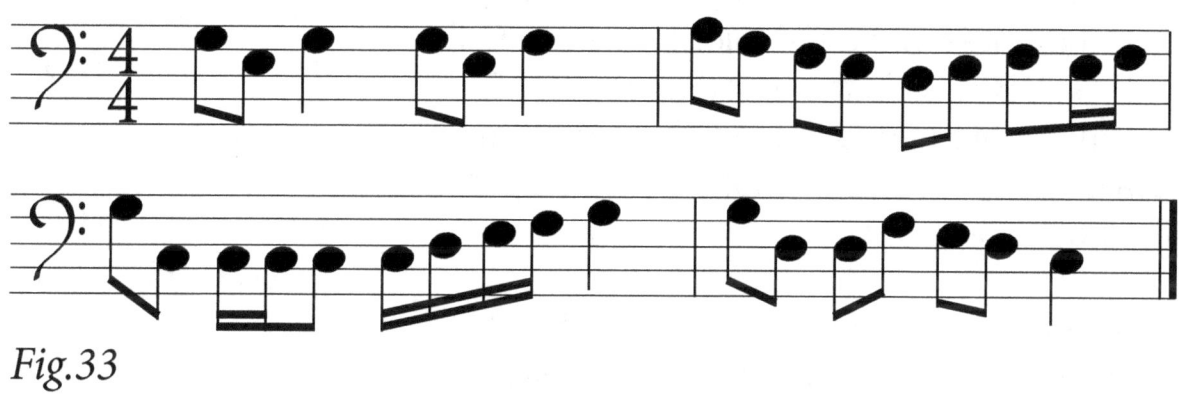

Fig.33

Then There's Ten

John Sebastian Gaskin
© 2013 BMI

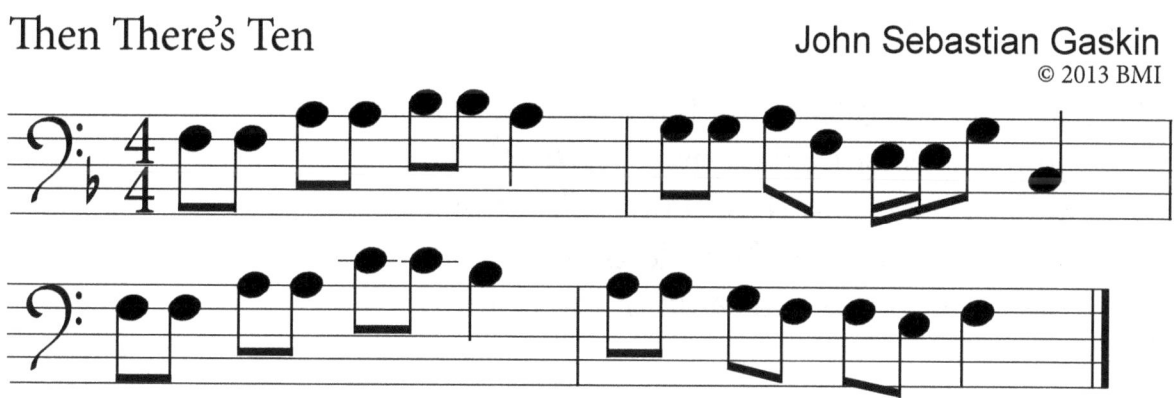

Fig.34

10 - Music Theory 102

This section teaches the theory of how chords are formed. We will look at the **Major** (M - Maj) and **Minor** (m - min) Chords. The bass guitar has evolved and bassists now play chords and solos along with their supportive role of keeping that pulse. Jaco did all this using a four string bass.

The **Chords** are built on the Root, Third and Fifth notes of the scale it represents (Fig.14 and Fig.15). The C-Major Scale has no sharp or flats. In the Music Theory section we see that the notes in the C-Major Scale are **C**-D-**E**-F-**G**-A-B-C. C is the first (Root) note, E is the third note and G is the fifth note of the scale. So the C-Major chord is made up of the notes C-E-G.

The G-Major Scale has one sharp (#). The notes in the G-Major Scale are **G**-A-**B**-C-**D**-E-F#-G. G is the first (Root) note, B is the third note and D is the fifth note of the scale. The G-Major chord is made up of the notes G-B-D.

The F-Major Scale has one flat (♭). The notes in the F-Major Scale are **F**-G-**A**-B♭-**C**-D-E-F. F is the first (Root) note, A is the third note and C is the fifth note of the scale. The F-Major chord is made up of the notes F-A-C.

In a Major Chord the interval between the first (root) note and the second note is a

"The root and third notes of a scale are all that is needed to give the quality of the chord. The third tells if the chord is major or minor."

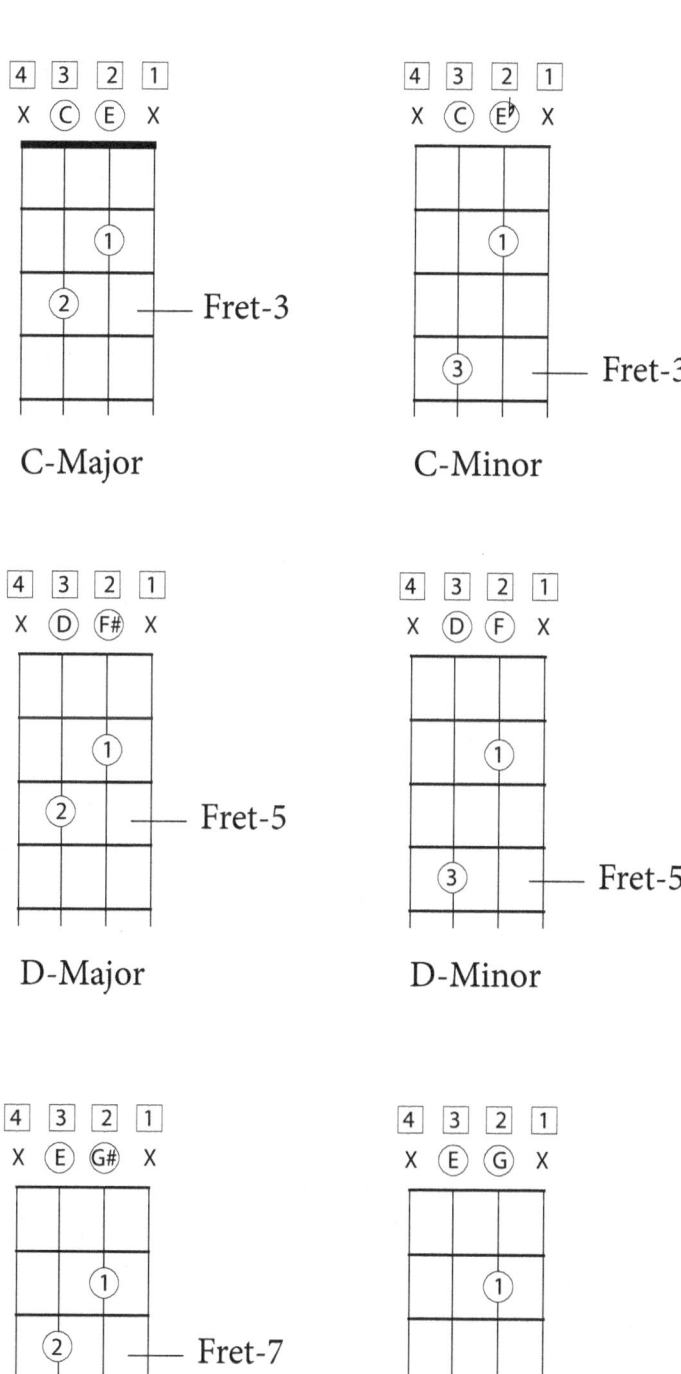

"The 'X' above the fretboard indicates that that string should not be played (muted). The notes above the fretboard are the notes in the chord being played."

'major third'. The interval between the first (root) note and the third note is a 'perfect fifth', shown in the Music Theory 101 section. C-Major can also be written CM or CMaj.

To create a Minor chord from a Major chord, lower the third note of the scale a half step. On the bass guitar that is moving back one fret, essentially flattening the note. C-Minor (Cm or Cmin) notes are C-E♭-G. In a Minor Chord the interval between the first (root) note and the second note is a **Minor Third**. The interval between the first (root) note and the third note remains a **Perfect Fifth**.

In the Music Theory 101 section we mentioned that there are no sharp or flats between the notes B-C and E-F. Again, they do occur. If one is to call out the notes in a D-Minor chord they will be D-F-A. If one asks for the notes of a D-flat Minor chord the notes will be D♭-F♭-A♭. Here we have an F♭ because we have to keep the designation of 'F' in the chord. If we called the note 'E' it would be referring to a chord other than D♭ Minor.

Two note chords (dyads), with the root note and the third, are shown. Major and Minor chords are shown moving down the fretboard. It is all about position playing and patterns which makes the bass easy to play.

"Two note chords are called dyads and three note chords are called triads. The root and the third for bassists are the basic chord structure used."

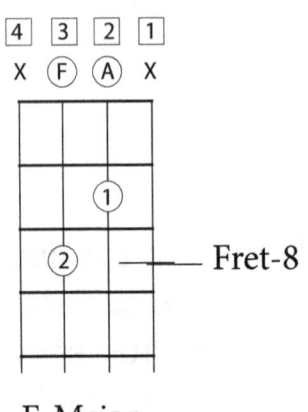

F-Major

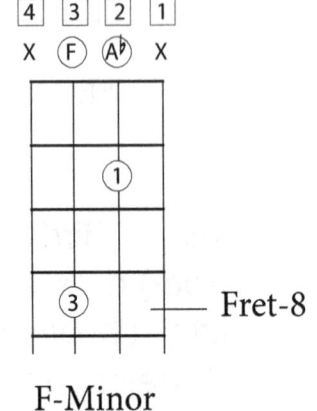

F-Minor

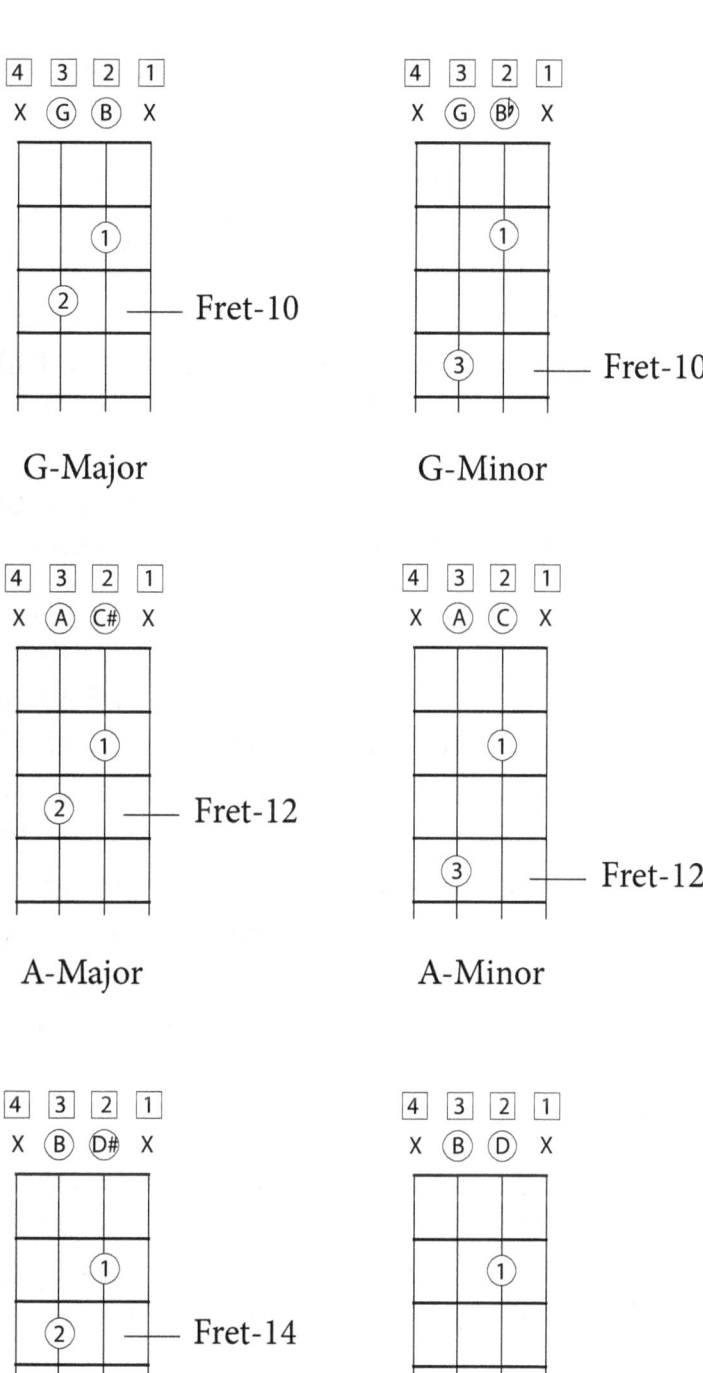

"The notes on the third string show the 'root' of the chord while the notes on the second string shows the 'third' making up the two note chord."

The reality and ease of position and pattern playing is that any change of key means that you will slide your left hand to another part of the fretboard (position) and play the same pattern as you were in the previous key.

Fig.35 show other two note chords, this time the notes are on the first and second strings. As before, move down the fretboard for other chords using the root note on the second string. As you progress, in understanding chords and in learning the fretboard, you will be able to find other two note chords on the fretboard. You will even find three note chords by adding the fifth note to the root and third notes you are already playing, Fig.36. You will notice in the triad examples the root note of the chords are not the lowest notes.

Now that you have an idea of how chords are formed we will now look at bass lines for chords. As mentioned previously, the root, third and fifth notes make up a triad (a three note chord). There are chords with more than three notes but we will not be looking at them in this book. Typical bass patterns are - the single note per chord pattern; the root, third and fifth; the root, fifth and octave; and octaves. We will look at Octaves in the Fretboard Basics 102 section. Sometimes the bass note follows the melodic notes on the first beat of a measure. There are many possibilities of bass patterns. In the three note pattern, if the chord is C-Major the bass will play the chords notes of C-E-G; G-Major will be G-B-D and A-Minor will be A-C-E, to name a few (Fig.14, Fig.15).

Exercise 1:
Fig.37 shows a four chord chart (C-F-Dm-G) in the treble staff. *Have a friend play the chords while you practice.* Below the treble staff is the bass staff. The simplest bass pattern to the chords shown would be to play one note (root note) per chord per measure as shown, typical for many ballads. So the notes to play are C-F-D-G. Shown below the bass staff is the tablature (tab) staff. This is a more fretboard like look at the notes. There are four lines representing the four strings on a typical bass guitar. The dividing lines represents the bar lines as in the other staves. The numbers on each string in the tab represents the fret and string to press. Thus 'C' is on the third fret of the third string. The notes written in the tab would be the same as if written on the other staves. Tablature is another way of writing and reading guitar parts. You may be at a session where the music is written only in 'tab' form, learn everything.

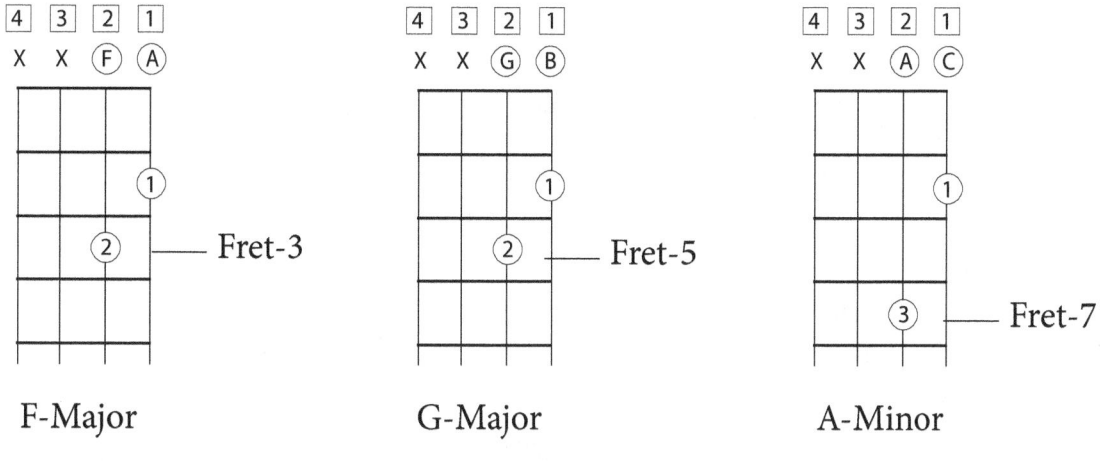

Fig.35

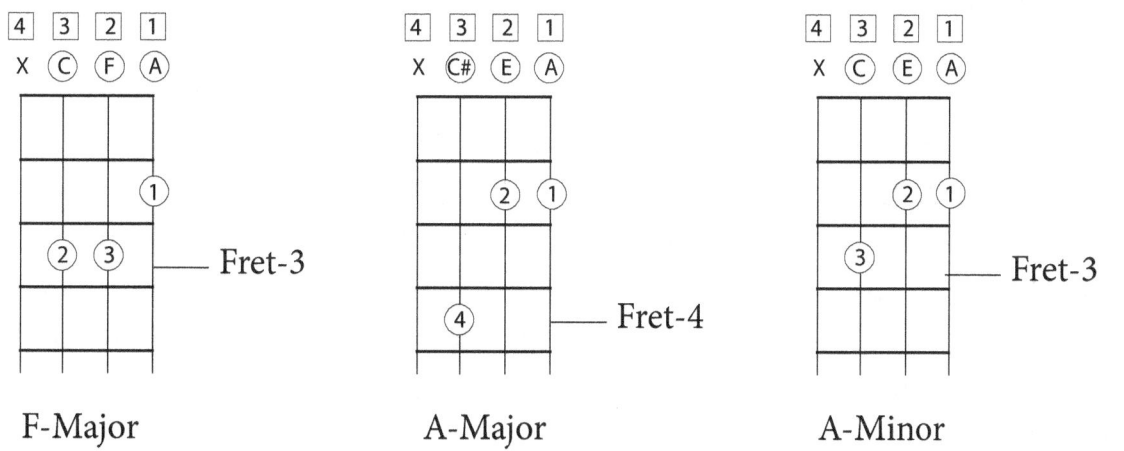

Fig.36

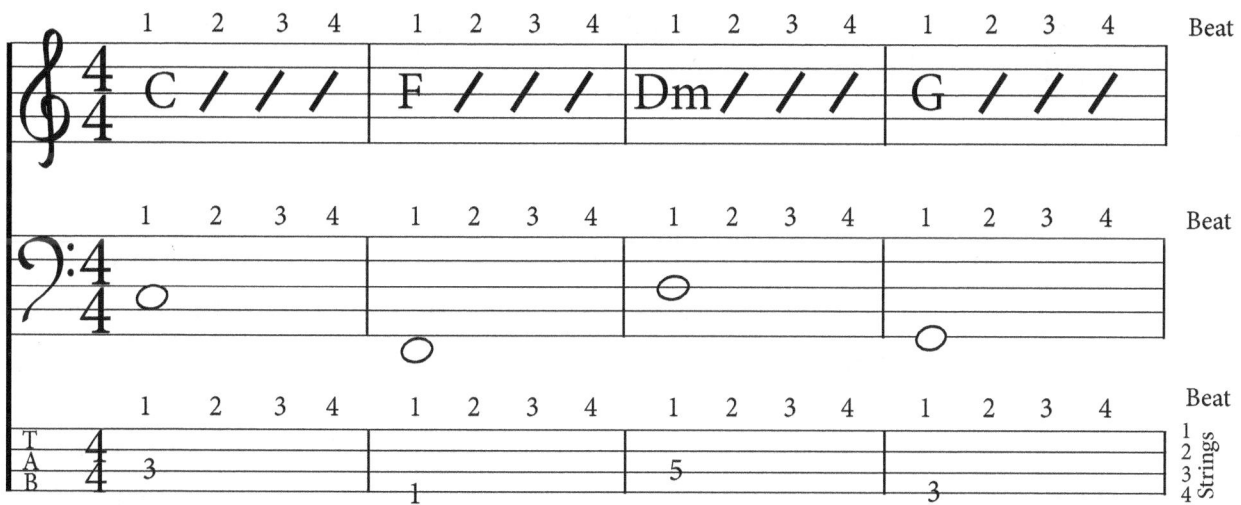

Fig.37

Exercise 2:
Fig.38 also shows the treble staff with the same chords as in exercise 1, a bass staff and a tab staff, except now the bass and tablature staves have more notes. This time there are four quarter notes per measure on the bass and tab staves with the same root note of the chord repeated. In exercise 1 it was not important to have you play alternating fingers with the right hand or down and up strokes with a pick. In this exercise it is important. With your right hand you will play the first and third notes with your index finger and alternate with your middle finger for the second and fourth notes (i-m-i-m), Fig.23. For those using a pick you will use a downstroke on the first and third notes and alternate using an upstroke on the second and fourth notes (down-up-down-up).

Exercise 3:
Fig.39 is similar to Fig.38 except the bass notes changes and you will be playing the root, third and fifth notes of the chord being represented. There is a C-Major chord and you will be playing the notes C-E-G, an F-Major chord F-A-C, a D-Minor chord D-F-A and a G-Major chord G-B-D. Since there are three notes in the chord and there are four notes in a measure, the third note will be repeated in each measure. This is sometimes referred to as an apeggiated bass line. Here again use alternate picking as in exercise 2 with the pick. We are going to get a bit classical playing with the fingers of the right hand. On the first note use the index finger, on the second note use the middle finger, on the third note use the ring finger and the middle finger again on the fourth note (i-m-a-m), Fig.23.

Exercise 4:
Fig.40 shows a chord progression on the treble staff. The first four chords in the progression is the same as you have been practicing in exercises 1-3. The second line has two new chords, E-minor and A-minor. You will practice this progression using the same ideas in exercises 1-3. You will first play one note per measure, the root note. Next you will play the root note four times in each measure and lastly, you will play the root, third, fifth and repeated third notes of each chord. See Fig.14 and Fig.15 and the beginning of this lesson.

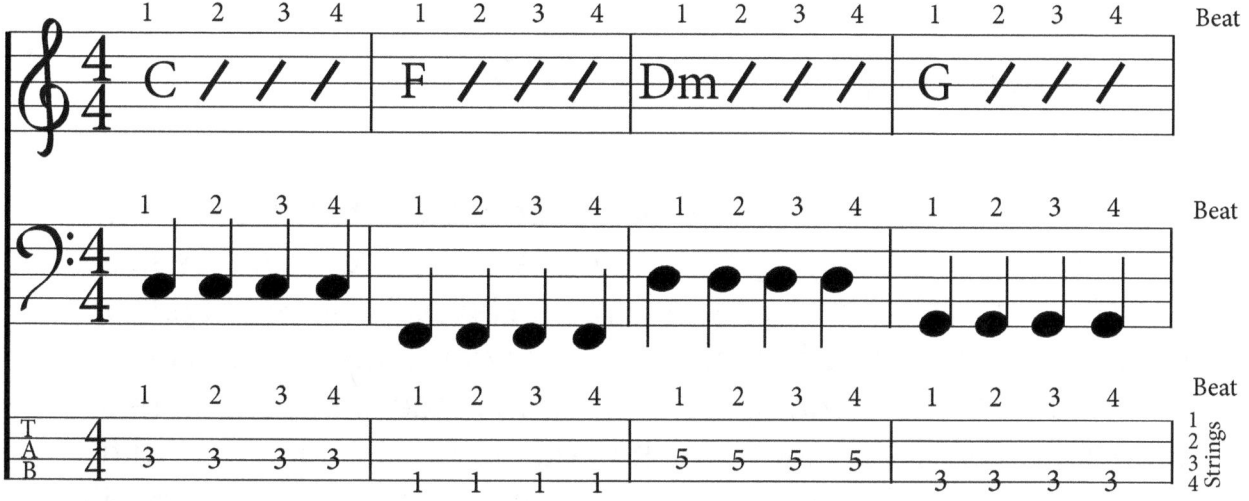

Fig.38

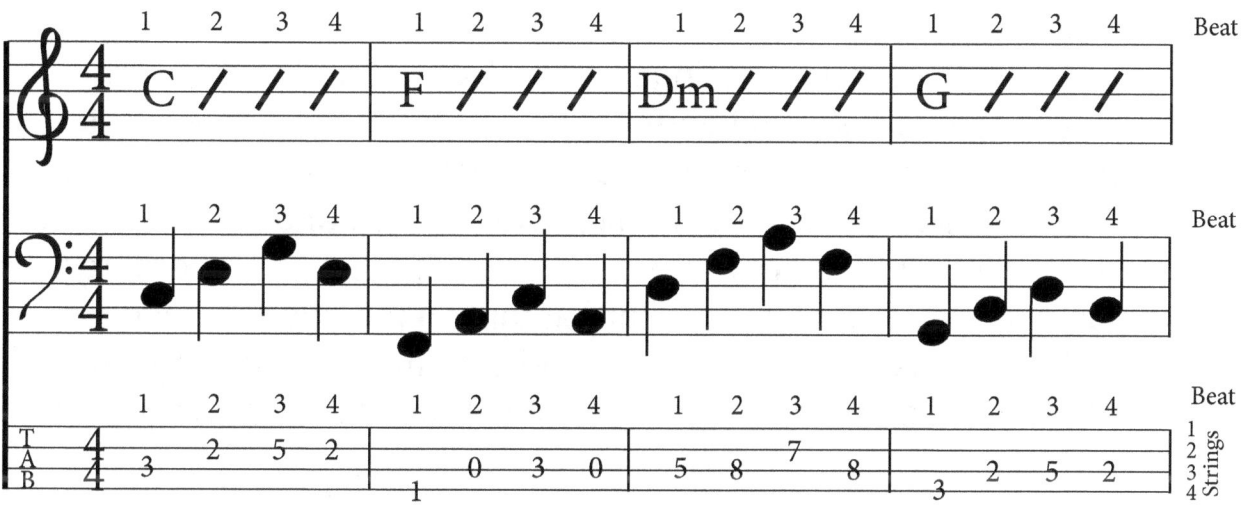

Fig.39

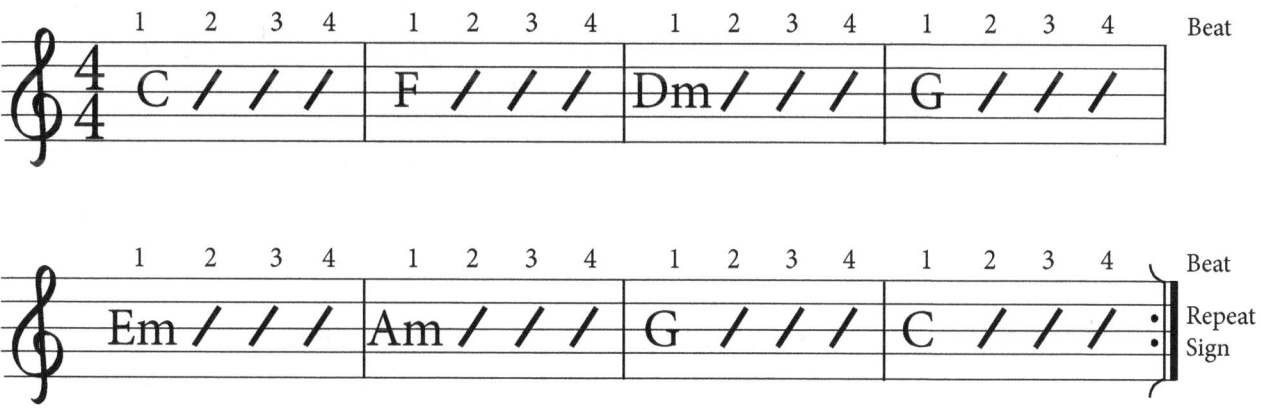

Fig.40

11 - Fretboard Basics 102

At this point the student should be comfortable with the bass guitar and playing. When playing the exercises in the Fretboard Basics 101 section your left hand fingers may have stayed bunched together to help support each other, now that changes. These exercises are to get you, the student, more independence with your fingers. Especially, your little finger, which needs to be strengthened with the others. So, with bass guitar tuned and metronome on - play the following exercises.

Exercise 1:
Using Fig.41 place your first finger at the first fret on the first string and play that note (G#). Put your second finger at the second fret, leaving your first finger in place and play that note (A). Put your third finger at the third fret, leaving the first two in place and play that note (A#). Put your fourth finger at the fourth fret, leaving the other three in place and play that note (B). Repeat this on the second, third and fourth strings. Reverse the exercise and play from the fourth string down to the first string again going from the first fret to the fourth fret.

Exercise 2:
Repeat exercise 1, going from the fifth fret to the eight on the first string up to the fourth string and back to the first string. Then try the twelfth fret to the fifteenth, again going up to the fourth string and back down to the first string, Fig.41A and Fig. 41B. The fret spaces get smaller as you go down the fretboard so you do not stretch out your fingers as you would have done at the first to fourth fret. This will give your finger a chance to feel out the bass guitar and also be more comfortable with the exercise.

Exercise 3:
In this exercise, the student will play one note per fret but with alternate fingering of the left hand, going from first string up to fourth, then back down to the first string. This time the students using

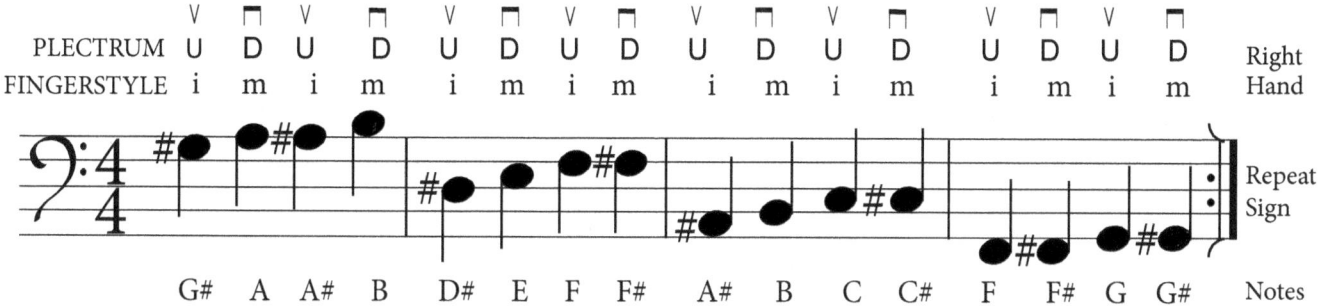

Fig.41

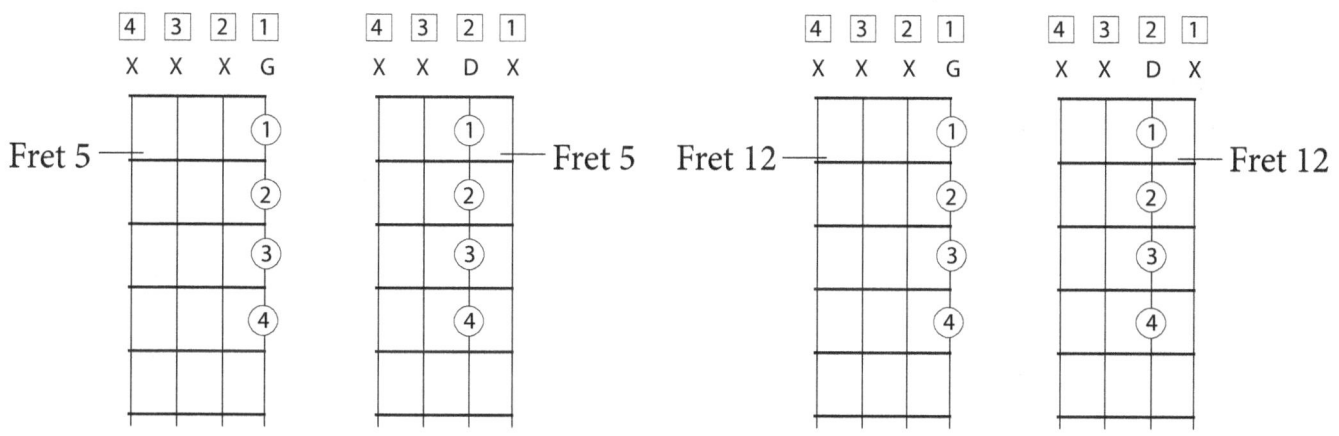

Fig.41A *Fig.41B*

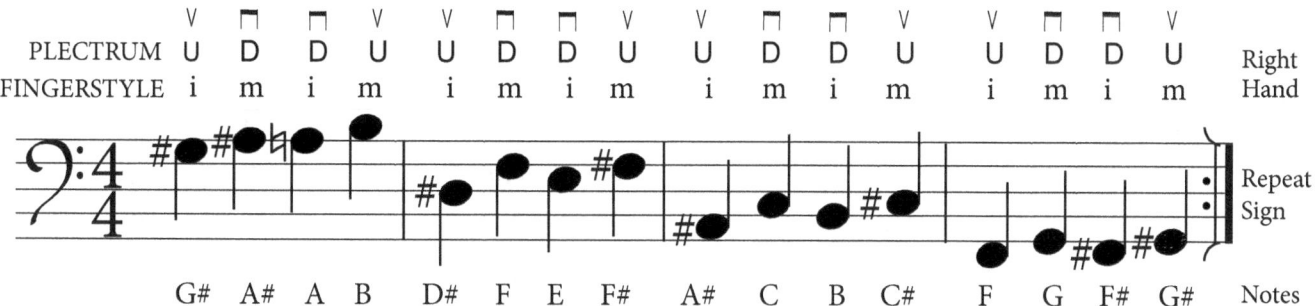

Fig.42

the plectrum shall use the picking technique of up-down-down-up. Those playing fingerstyle will continue to use the two fingers of their right hand, the index and middle, for the exercise as indicated in Fig.42.

Now, we will start practicing **Scales** using the first five frets of the bass guitar. The root note of each scale has been grayed out. These exercises will employ, alternating down-up strokes, with the plectrum and alternating between index and middle fingers for fingerstyle players. These exercises will go from the fourth string down to the first string and back up to the fourth string.

Exercise 4:
Using Fig.43 and Fig.43A this exercise is to practice the G-Major Scale, starting on the third fret on the fourth string, with the root note of the scale, 'G'. This scale has one sharp, F#. This 'G' note is located on the bottom line of the musical bass staff. This scale position is referred to as the - first position, fourth string, G-Major.

Exercise 5:
Using Fig.44 and Fig.44A this exercise is the C-Major Scale, starting on the third fret on the third string, with the root note of the scale, 'C'. This scale has no sharps or flats, all notes are natural. This note is the 'C' in the staff. This scale position is referred to as the - first position, fifth string, C-Major. This scale only goes one octave as we are just playing on the first five frets.

Exercise 6:
Using Fig.45 and Fig.45A this exercise is the A-Minor Scale, starting on the fifth fret of the fourth string. If one compares this scale to the C-Major scale in Fig.44 and Fig.44A, you will notice that it has the same notes. The difference is that this scale starts on the scale root note of 'A'. A-minor is the relative minor of C-Major, which means literally that they are related. 'A' is the sixth scale degree (note) of the C-Major scale and is referred to as the Aeolian Scale or Relative Minor Scale. Other minor scales are the Minor Pentatonic (blues), Harmonic and Melodic. We will not be looking at them in this book.

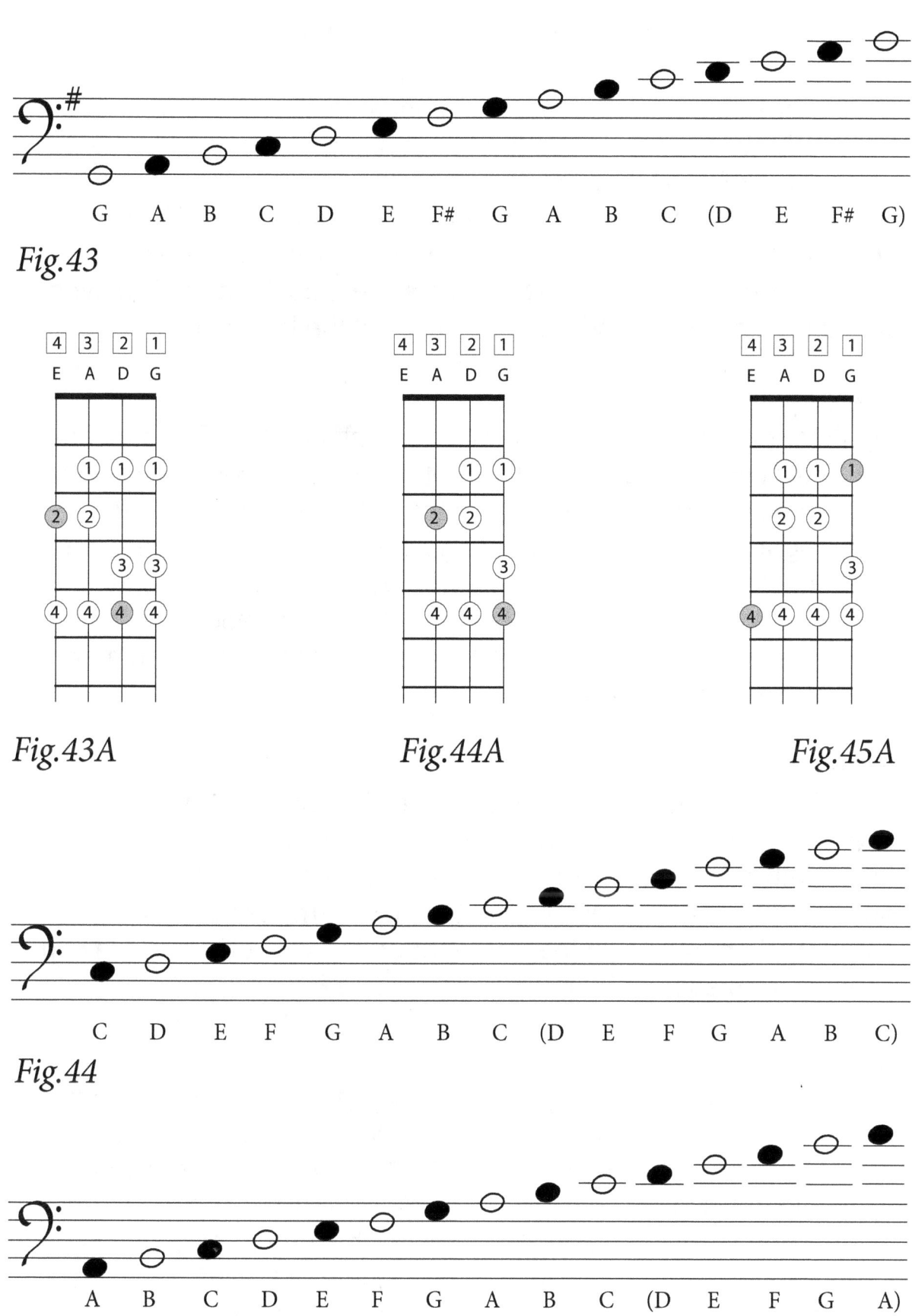

The **Octaves** we will be looking at here are the two note octaves. That is, the same note but of different pitches, eight notes apart. On the bass guitar they occur two strings apart and two frets apart. Fig.46 shows the note 'F' on the fourth string at the first fret. Its octave, a higher pitched 'F', occurs on the second string at the third fret (two strings and two frets apart). Fig.47 shows the B♭ octave, with the low B♭ on the third string at the first fret and the higher B♭ on the first string at the third fret. Octaves are most commonly played with the index finger and the third finger of the left hand.

Exercise 7:
Fig.46 shows octaves on 'F', a musical staff and tab. The staff has the 'F' for two beats each on the root and octave. With the pick play both notes with downstrokes. With the index and middle fingers of the right hand play an alternating pattern (i-m-i-m). Repeat until comfortable, then move down the fretboard two frets to the 'G' octaves and play, then two frets to the 'A' octaves and play. Move down the fretboard up to the twelfth fret, playing octaves from each note of the F-Major scale, see Fig.14.

Exercise 8:
Fig.47 shows octaves on B♭. With the pick play down-up strokes alternating. With the fingers of the right hand play the low note with the thumb and the higher note with the index finger the first time and the middle finger the second time (P-i-P-m), repeat. When comfortable move down the fretboard up to the twelfth fret, playing octaves from each note of the B♭ scale, see Fig.14.

Exercise 9:
Fig.48 shows the same progression we saw in the Music Theory 102 section. In this exercise we will be practicing another common pattern of bassists using octaves. The bass pattern for the chords shown in this exercise will be root-fifth-octave-fifth. The tablature section shows which fret to play and which string to play. In this exercise use the first, third and fourth fingers of the left hand. Using the pick alternate down-up strokes. Using fingers of the right hand alternate between the index, middle and the ring fingers, i-m-a-m.

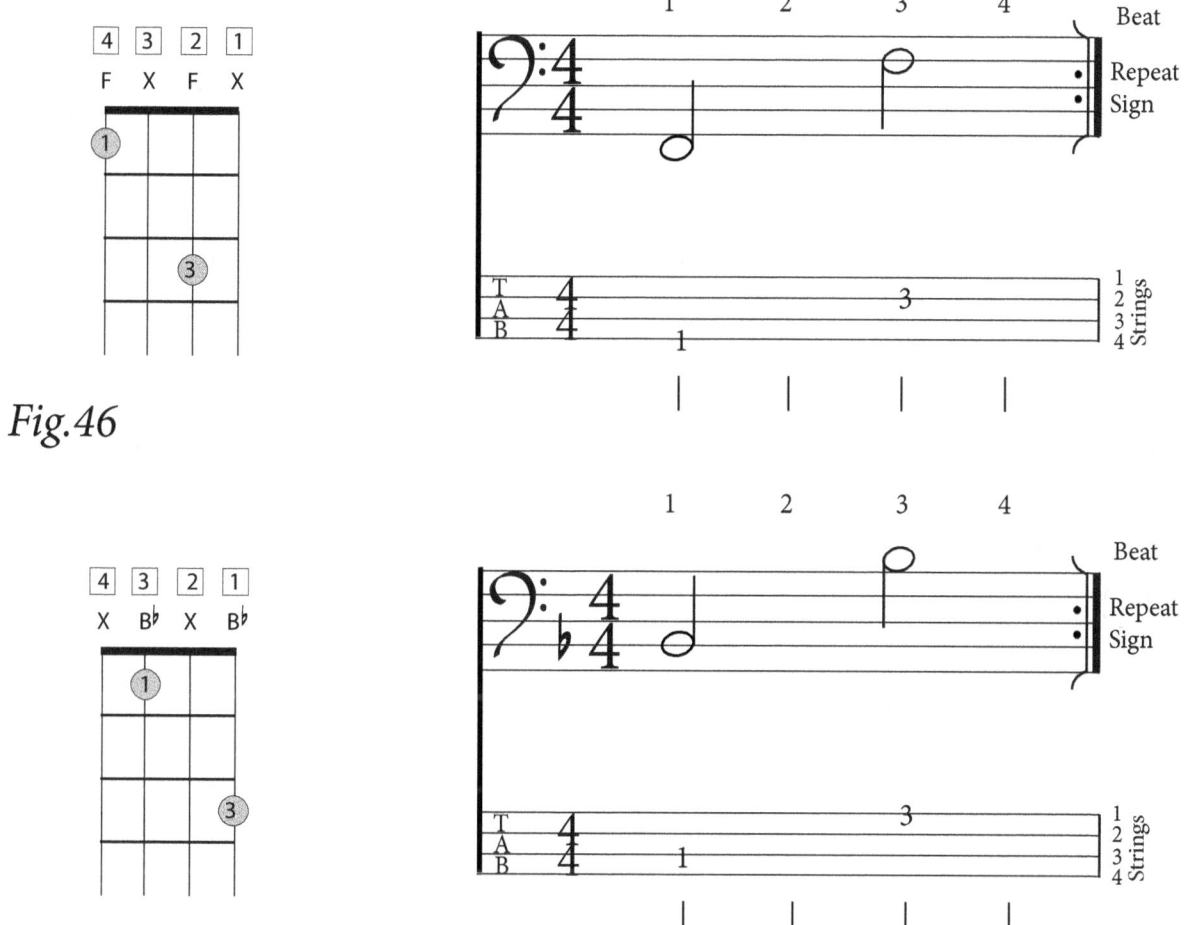

Fig.46

Fig.47

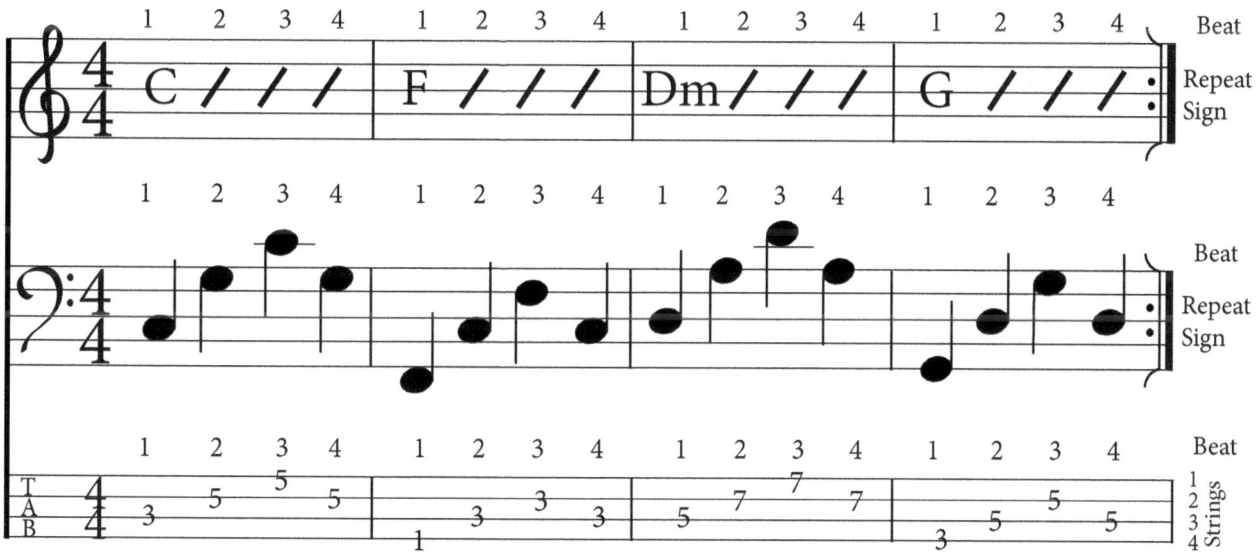

Fig.48

12 - Rhythmic Training 102

It is very important to be able to play a bass pattern with a consistent rhythm and timing, not to be robotic but to make sure that groove 'sits in the pocket', as they say. Again, this is where practicing with a metronome is very important, put the speed on 40 to start. The notes played should be even in volume, tone, timing and feel, unless stated otherwise. Patience, concentration and persistence are the watchwords. It may seem tedious at times but once you get it, **you get it.** Start slowly and gradually speed up your metronome as your playing improves and you get more comfortable with the exercises. They will start off simple as you would have already practiced some of the patterns. This section is not about the note(s) you will be playing but how you play it/them.

Exercise 1:
Fig.49 shows quarter notes in the measure. It is the same note 'A', fourth string fifth fret. As you have the metronome set on 40, play each quarter note together with each beat of the metronome. Alternate down-up picking with the pick (plectrum). Alternate index and middle fingers plucking with the right hand. With the left hand press the note with your index (1) finger. When you have 'become one with the metronome' alternate fingers of the left hand. That is, start with the index finger (1) for the first note then use the middle finger (2) for the second time you play the note, the ring finger (3) for the third time and the little finger (4) for the fourth time. When repeating start with the little finger going back to the index finger.

Exercise 2:
Fig.50 shows eight notes in the measure. There are now two notes per beat. Use the same ideas for the right and left hand as in exercise 1 to play this exercise. The second note occurs between the beats of the metronome.

Exercise 3:
Fig.51 shows sixteenth notes in the measure. There are now four notes per beat. Use the same ideas as in exercise 1.

Fig.49

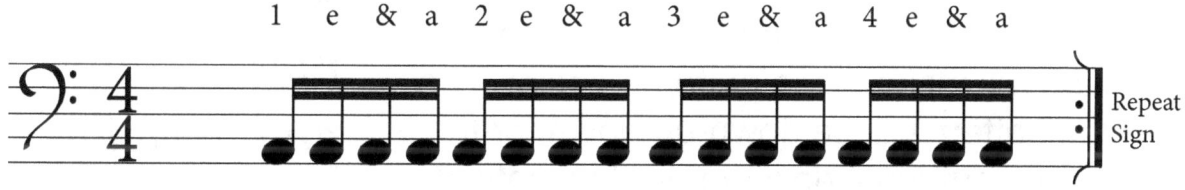

Fig.50

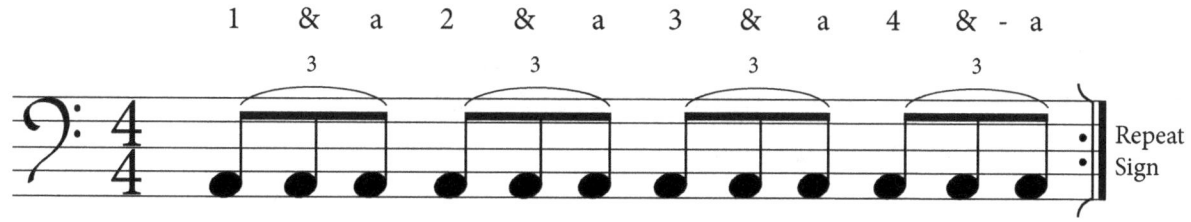

Fig.51

Fig.52

Exercise 4:
Fig.52 shows a new pattern, **Triplets**. Triplets are three notes together with a tie at the top with the number three. They could be of any value. There are now three notes per beats. For this exercise you will use a down-up-down picking pattern for each set of triplets. The right hand fingering will be i-m-a for each set of triplets. Use a different finger of the left hand for each sets of triplets (for each beat) starting with the index going to the little finger.

Exercise 5:
Fig.53, Fig.54, Fig.55 and Fig.56 again show sixteenth notes in the measure. This time a sixteenth note is missing in each beat and in its place a rest. When three notes are together they act like triplets but the rhythm is different. Hopefully, by now you would have a clear grasp of the sixteenth note pattern. So, concentration and slow practice will make these patterns easier. The picking pattern will be down-up-down for the three note patterns, down-up for two note patterns and down for single notes. Right hand fingering will be i-m-a for three note patterns, i-m for two note patterns and 'i' for single notes. For every beat use a different finger of the left hand starting with the little finger going back to the index finger. When repeating start with the index finger going to the little finger of the left hand for every beat. *Take your time* to get it right.

As mentioned before, it is very important to develop the little finger of your left hand.

"It is very important to practice using your little finger on the left hand. It will allow you more options and flexibility when you are playing."

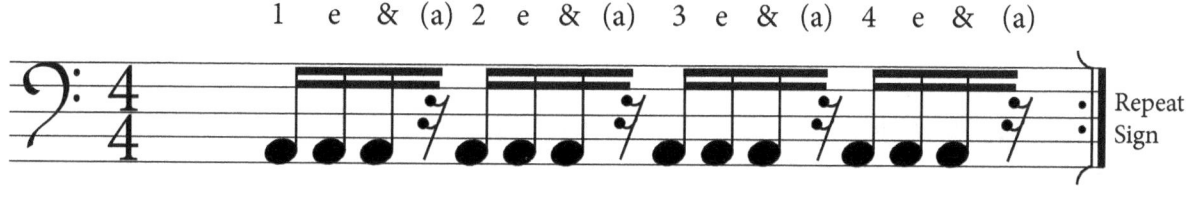

Fig.53

Fig.54

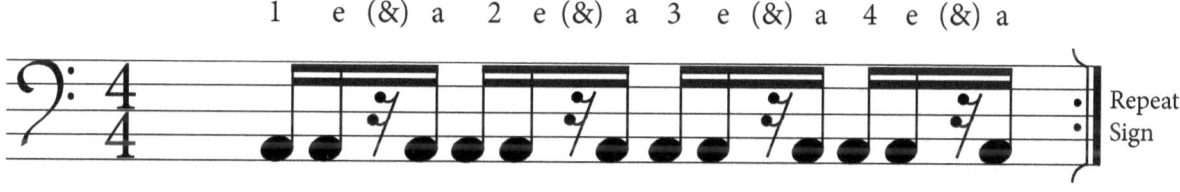

Fig.55

Fig.56

13 - Music Theory 103

In the Music Theory 101 section we learnt the intervals of a major scale. **Chords** that are built from the root, fourth or fifth tones (scale degrees) of a major scale will always produce Major chords. Chords built from the second, third or sixth tones of the major scale produce Minor chords. Chords built from the seventh tone of a major scale produces a **Diminished** chord. The scale degree tone the chord is built from becomes the root of that chord.

The seventh of a B♭ scale is A (Fig.15, Music Theory 101 section). A chord built on 'A' will give the notes A-C-E♭, an A-Diminished chord. In a Diminished Chord the interval between the first (root) note and the second note is a 'minor third'. The interval between the first (root) note and the third note is a 'tritone', flatted fifth. The Diminish Chord is seen as a minor chord with the fifth flattened. There are two intervals of minor thirds (three semi-tones) between the notes.

Diminished chords, normally resolve or, move to the one (root) chord, which is aided by the leading tone of the scale moving to be resolved. In the C-Major scale the B (seventh note) resolves to the C (root). In this case the seventh note resolves up to the octave. The Diminished Chord seems to function like a Dominant Chord (chords built on the fifth scale degree). They both want to go to another chord to resolve.

"The lowest note of any chord can be any note of that chord. When a different note other than the root occur in the bass, the chords is said to be inverted."

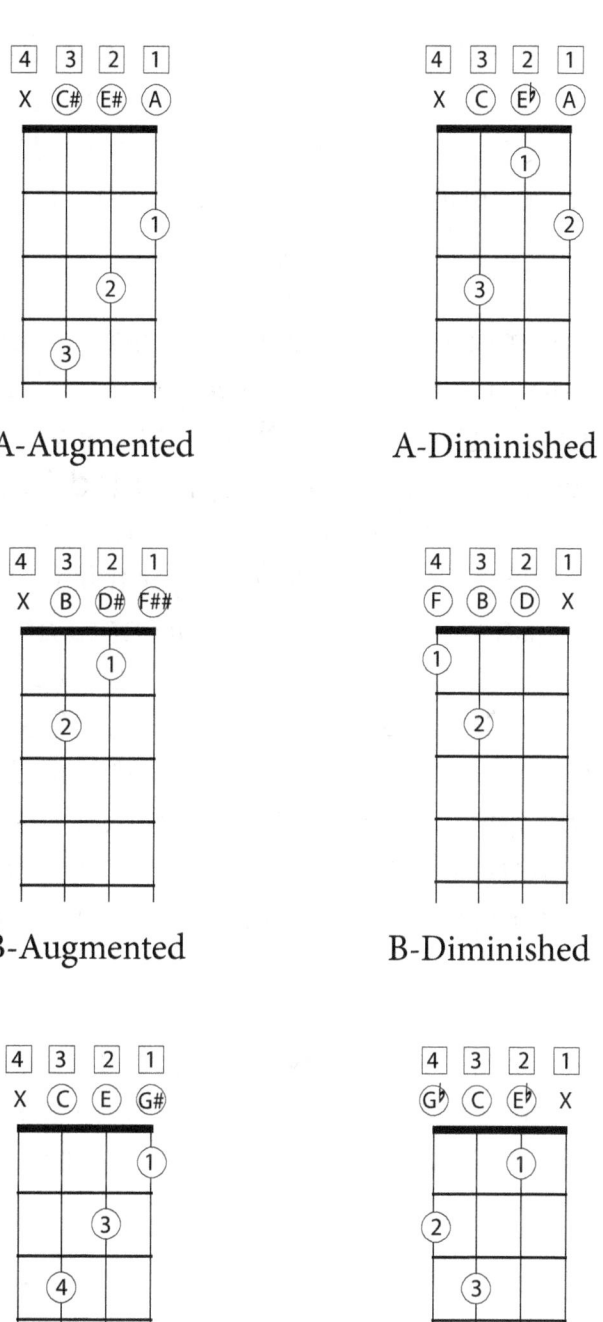

"Diminished Chords are considered a type of Minor Chord, and Augmented Chords are considered a type of Major Chord."

All chords in this section shall be shown on the first five frets of the bass guitar. Once you know your fretboard enough you can move down the fretboard to the twelfth fret to play higher notes.

53

The Diminished and Augmented chords have unique sounds. They create tension and they sound unresolved. They need to go to another chord to finish 'the idea'. They are used mainly as passing chords.

The Augmented Chord is not part of the scale degree theory. An Augmented Chord built from the note F of the B♭ scale will give the notes F-A-C#. In an Augmented Chord the interval between the first (root) note and the second note is a 'major third'. The interval between the first (root) note and the third note is a 'augmented fifth', sharpened fifth. The C# note is not in the key of B♭. The Augmented chord is seen as a Major Chord with the fifth sharpened, or moved up a semi-tone. There are two intervals of major thirds, four semi-tones (two whole tones) between the notes.

Modern day music have accepted these chords and have used them in different ways other than a resolution to other chords.

"Leading Tones are notes of the seventh scale degree that are a half-step away from the tonic note it resolves towards."

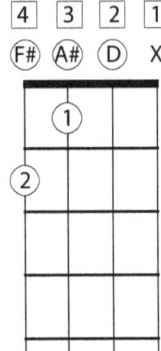

D-Augmented

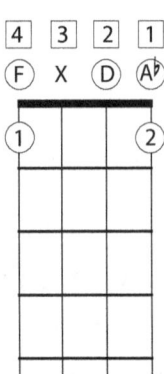

D-Diminished

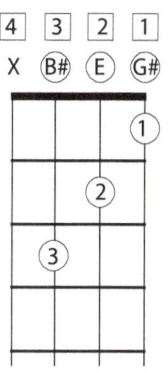

E-Augmented

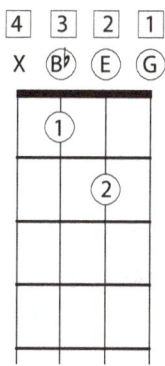

E-Diminished

"In the early years of music the Diminished Chord was considered 'Devil Music'. It created a dissonant sound, a tritone interval, that was not accepted."

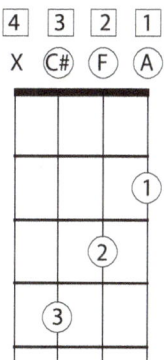

F-Augmented

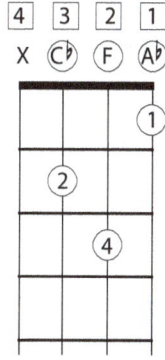

F-Diminished

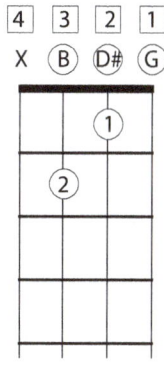

G-Augmented

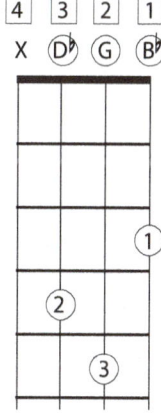

G-Diminished

When practicing these chords make sure that the changes, from one chord to the another, is smooth and even. You have learnt the four chord qualities of the triad; Major, Minor, Augmented and Diminished.

14 - Songs

Congratulations, you have come to the end of Bass Guitar-1. Hopefully, you have made much progress in your learning to play the bass, in music theory and sight reading. You can always go back over material in this book as you need to. You can now increase the speed of the metronome to where you would be most comfortable. As an exercise you can even set the metronome to much faster speeds to see if you can play correctly at those speeds.

Here are some songs for you to practice with chords and with the melody in the bass clef. Once you have learnt a melody you can get adventurous. Find the lead note on another part of the fretboard and basically play the same pettern as you did before. You have already learnt to add bass patterns based on chords in the Music Theory 102 section, which you can also apply to these songs. You can also obtain music sheets of songs you like to learn and play them.

Enjoy.

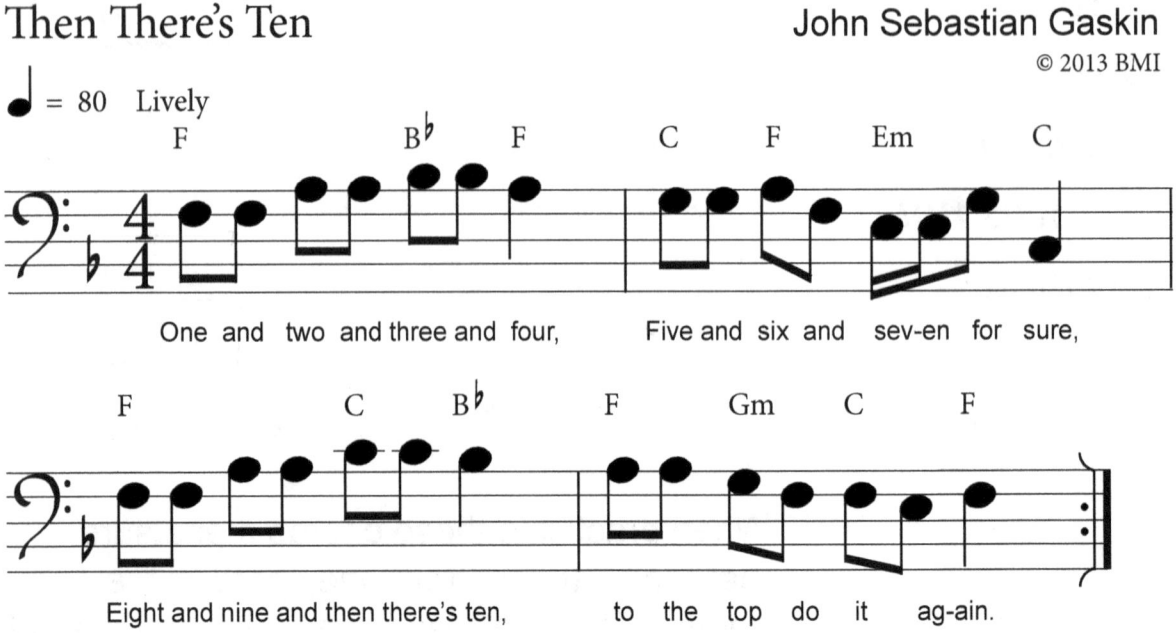

Fig.57

London Bridge

Claes Van Visscher
1616

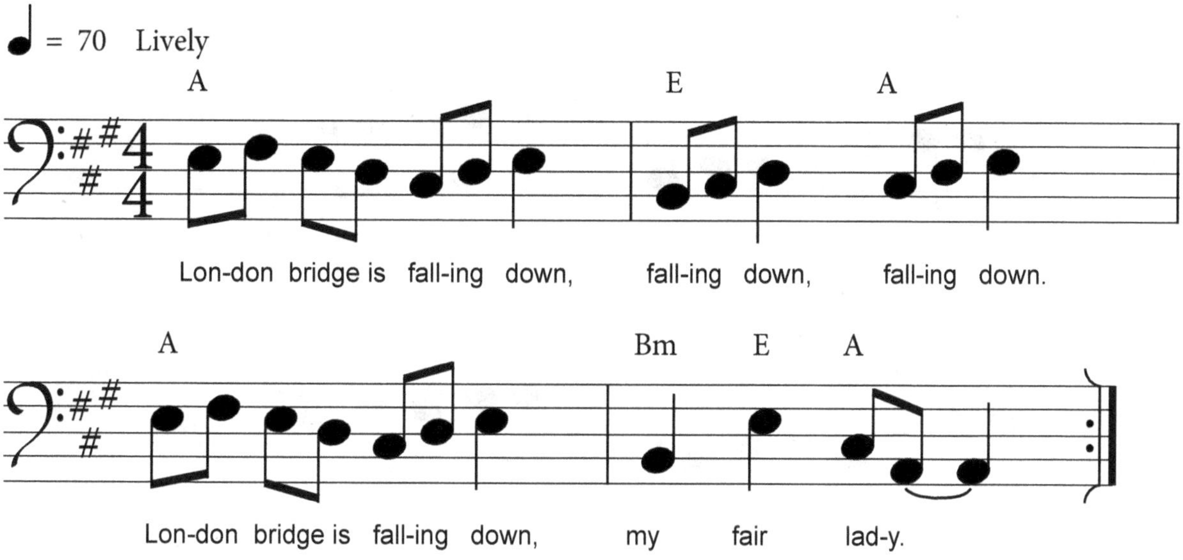

♩ = 70 Lively

Lon-don bridge is fall-ing down, fall-ing down, fall-ing down.
Lon-don bridge is fall-ing down, my fair lad-y.

Fig.58

I Saw Three Ships

arr: John S. Gaskin
1833 - Originally in 6/8 timing

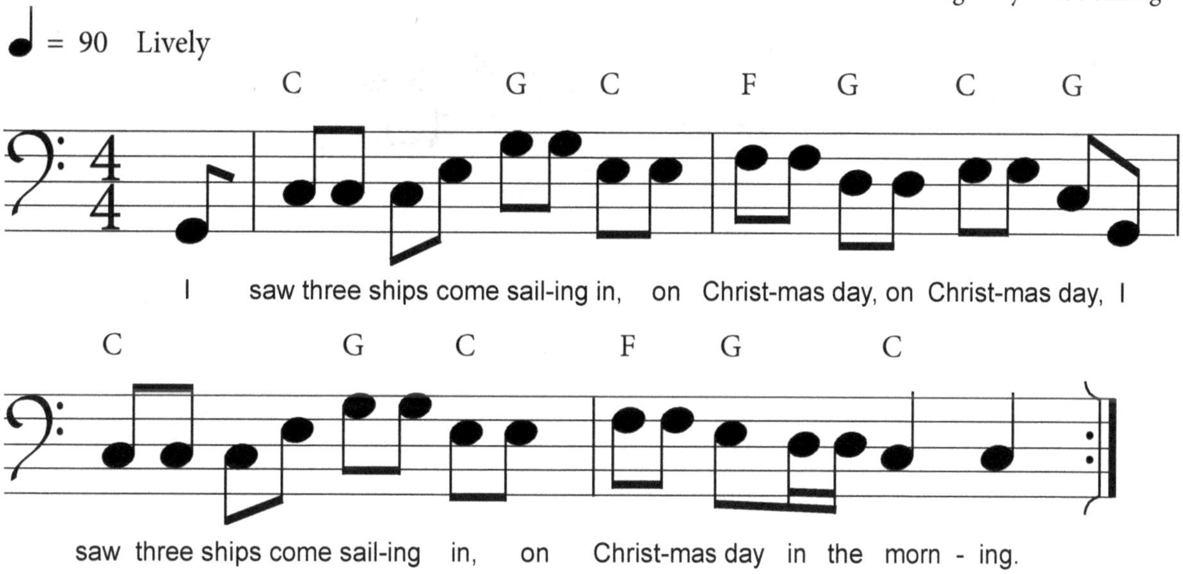

♩ = 90 Lively

I saw three ships come sail-ing in, on Christ-mas day, on Christ-mas day, I
saw three ships come sail-ing in, on Christ-mas day in the morn - ing.

Fig.59

Old MacDonald Had A Farm

Traditional
1917

♩ = 70 Lively

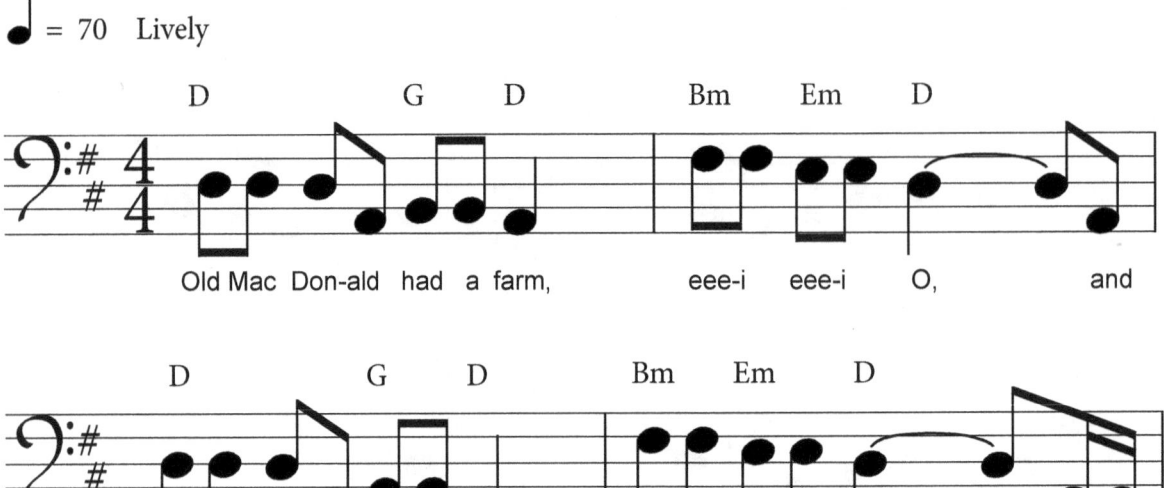

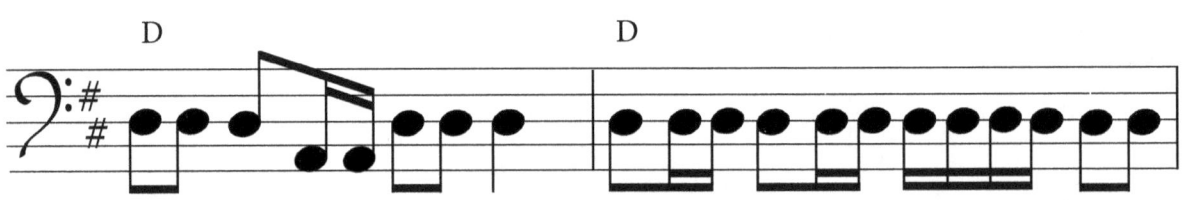

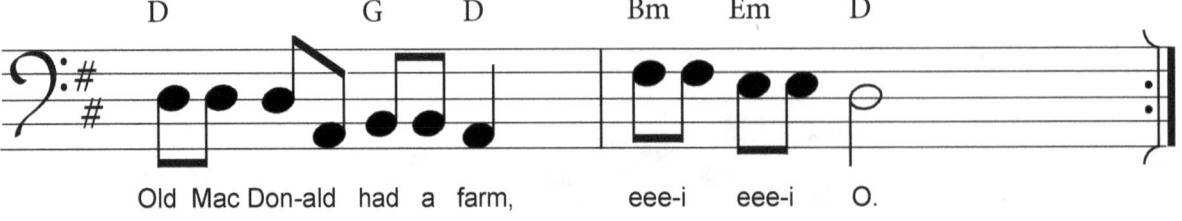

Fig.60

Mary Had A Little Lamb

Lowell Mason
1830

Fig.61

This Old Man

George Arthur Meyer
1906

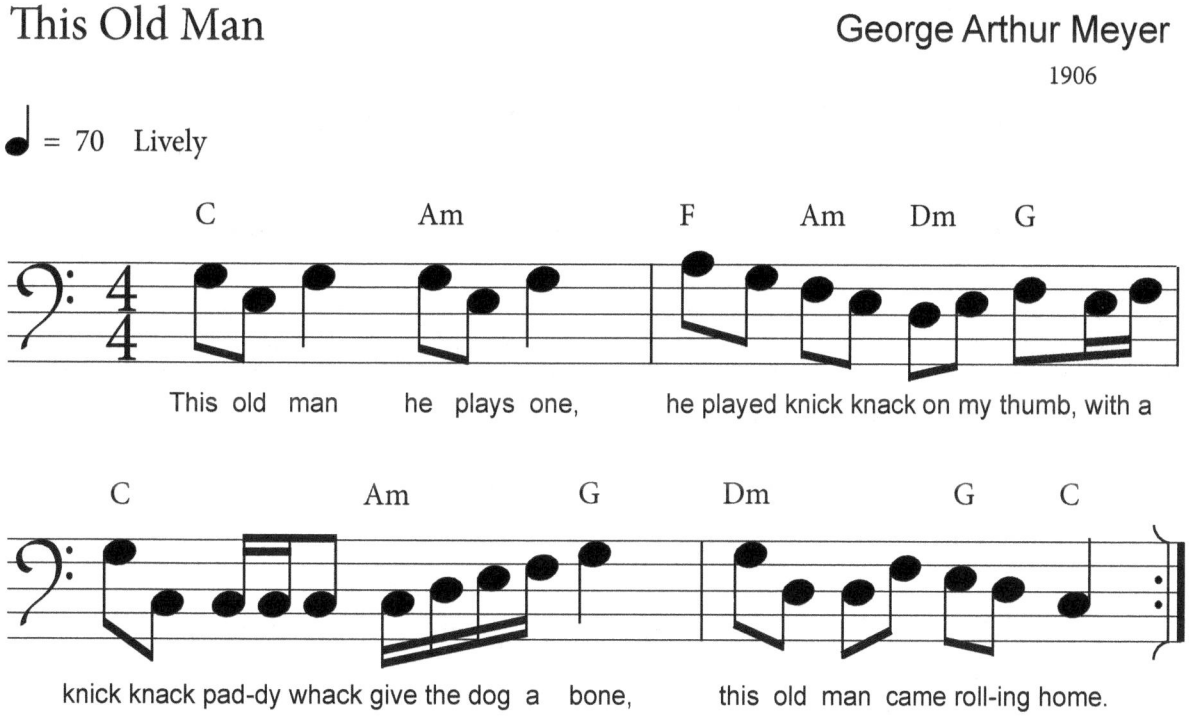

Fig.62

Baa Baa Black Sheep

Traditional
1744

♩ = 80 Lively

Fig.63

We Three Kings

John H. Hopkins
1857

♩ = 70 Lively

Fig.64

Jingle Bells

James Pierpont
1857

♩ = 70   Lively

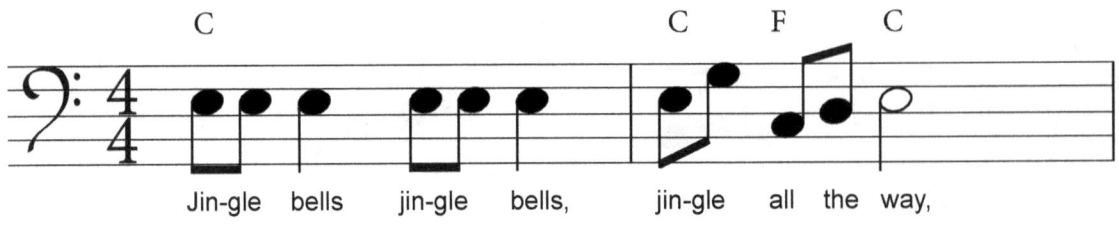

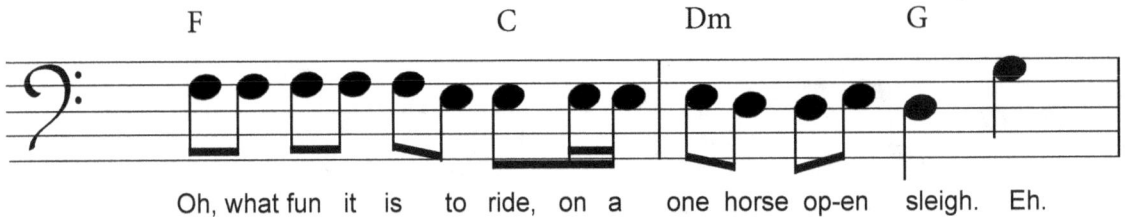

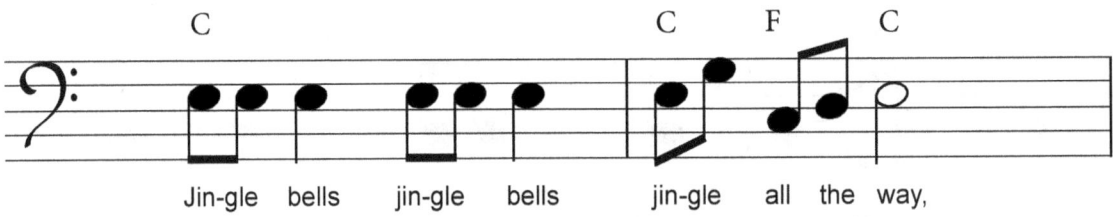

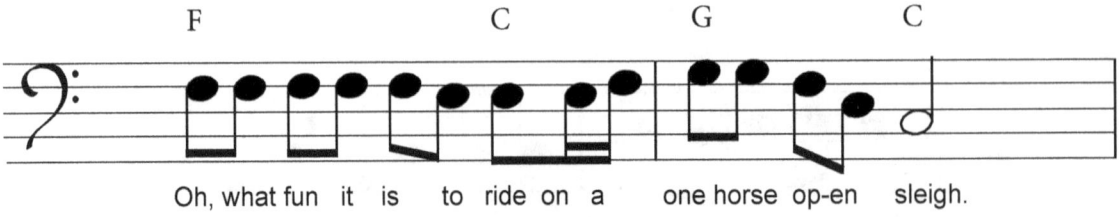

Fig.65

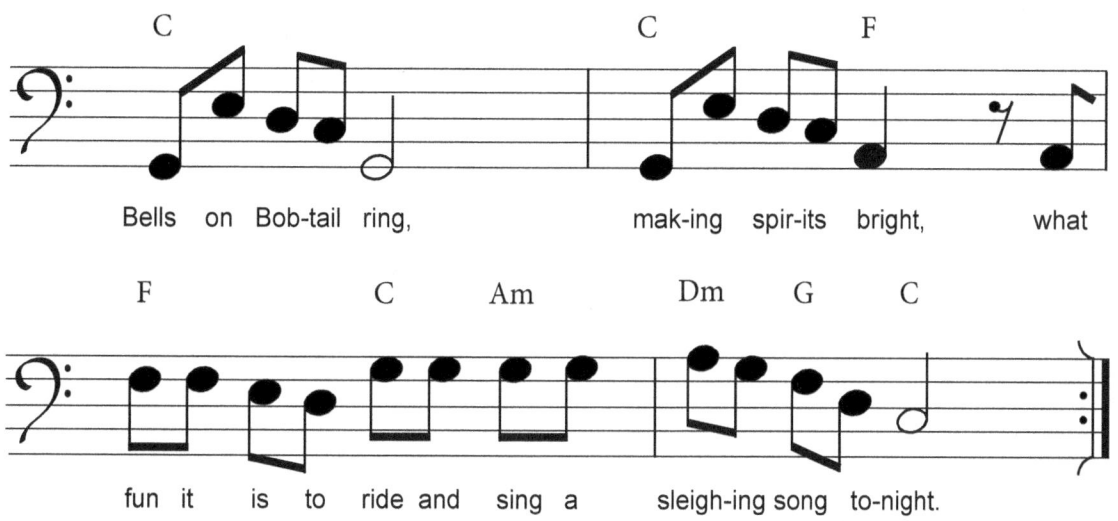

Fig.65 (con't.)

Twinkle Twinkle Little Star

Jane Taylor
1806

Fig.66

Rock-A-Bye Boo

John Sebastian Gaskin
© 2002 BMI

Fig.67

There are compositions with 6/8 time signature, in which there are six eight notes per measure. In some compositions you will not see six eight notes but the values of each measure adds up to six eight notes. When the beat is indicated in 6/8 timing and dotted quarter notes are used then the rhythm has a two beats per measure feel, where three eight notes are included in each beats (Fig.68). Keep the metronome very slow to beat each eight note, feel the beats.

Pop Goes The Weasel

Traditional
1855

♩. = 110 Lively

Fig.68

This is the end of **Bass-1: Beginning Bass Guitar-Music Theory-Sight Reading.** I hope that you are eager to continue your growth in your bass guitar playing and music. Practice is key. Get some songs you like, listen to them and try to pick out the bass lines. Get together with other musicians and jam. You will learn a lot from other musicians.

15 - References

Images courtesy of **John Sebastian Gaskin** (except as indicated)

Acoustic Upright Bass Guitar courtesy GHmusic.com

Electric Bass Guitar - **Ibanez SR300** courtesy of Ibanez.com

Tuners - **Korg CA-30**;
Korg Pitchclip Tuner courtesy of korg.com

Metronomes - **Zen-on Metrina**;
SX Metronome courtesy of edequity.com

Image of John Gaskin courtesy of Clayton Philip

All songs shown are in the public domain, except for '**Then There's Ten**' and '**Rock-A-Bye Boo**' written by **John Sebastian Gaskin**

Recommended Books:

Randel, D. M. (1978). *Harvard Concise Dictionary of Music*. Harvard University Press. Belknap Press. Cambridge, Mass.

Starer, R. (1969). *Rhythmic Training*. Universal - MCA Music Publishing Inc. Hal Leonard Publishing. New York, N.Y.

Self-Notes

Self-Notes

John Sebastian Gaskin

John Sebastian Gaskin is a musician, composer and now author. He has performed in New York, New Jersey, Connecticut, Delaware, Philadelphia, Trinidad and Tobago. He has studied music at Brooklyn College, New York. He studied guitar starting with Anthony 'Pimpa' Springer in Trinidad and with Steve Adelson in Brooklyn, New York.

"My very first instrument was a Japanese made 'Fender Jazz' styled bass guitar, but I could not find anyone who taught bass guitar. So, I learnt guitar and transferred some of the teaching and principles to the bass."

"I have made mention of Robert Starer earlier in the book. Robert Starer and Noah Creshevsky are two of my music teachers at Brooklyn College, who saw something in me, believed in me and encouraged me to believe in myself and my ability."

Other Book in the Series:
Guitar-1 Beginning: Guitar - Music Theory - Sight Reading.
Guitar-2 Intermediate: Guitar - Music Theory - Sight Reading.
Piano-1 Beginning: Piano - Music Theory - Sight Reading.

©-2016 Jo-Kin Music - BMI

BASS-1
©-2016 Jo-Kin Music - BMI

ISBN: 978-976-95914-0-0

www.ingramcontent.com/pod-product-compliance
Lightning Source LLC
Chambersburg PA
CBHW081327040426

42453CB00013B/2326